Cut The Anchor

Soar to Your Highest Potential by Releasing the Weight from Your Past

Kari Berridge

First published by Ultimate World Publishing 2023
Copyright © 2023 Kari Berridge

ISBN

Paperback: 978-1-923123-00-7
Ebook: 978-1-922982-99-5

Kari Berridge has asserted her rights under the Copyright, Designs and Patents Act 1988 to be identified as the author of this work. The information in this book is based on the author's experiences and opinions. The publisher specifically disclaims responsibility for any adverse consequences which may result from use of the information contained herein. Permission to use information has been sought by the author. Any breaches will be rectified in further editions of the book.

All rights reserved. No part of this publication may be reproduced, stored in or introduced into a retrieval system, or transmitted in any form, or by any means (electronic, mechanical, photocopying, recording or otherwise) without the prior written permission of the author. Any person who does any unauthorized act in relation to this publication may be liable to criminal prosecution and civil claims for damages. Enquiries should be made through the publisher.

Cover design: Ultimate World Publishing
Layout and typesetting: Ultimate World Publishing
Editor: Marnae Kelly
Cover Image Copyrights:
Romolo Tavani-Shutterstock.com
jnumber9-Shutterstock.com
i am adventure-Shutterstock.com

Ultimate World Publishing
Diamond Creek,
Victoria Australia 3089
www.writeabook.com.au

TESTIMONIALS

Kari is a caring and adventurous soul who has persevered with ruthless determination and undaunted courage to boost her confidence and overcome the demons, both personal and physical, that have dogged her past and threatened her future. Her story is a testament to her resilience and desire to let go of the past so that she may soar into a beautiful new world, all the better for her being a part of it.

Dawna Scrivens
BCom

Cut The Anchor

A friendship that began more than twenty years ago when our children attended the same elementary school together has been a blessing. Our paths have crossed often, leading to a deep bond built on shared interests and experiences. I deeply admire her authenticity, integrity, and relentless dedication to her goals. Our time together is truly rewarding, as her openness and candor are both refreshing and motivating. Kari's unwavering determination to tackle challenges is admirable, and her ability to adapt is inspiring. I have no doubt her exceptional traits will be a guiding light for others facing their journeys.

Tracy Spilde

In hearing of Kari's journey, it is truly amazing what she has overcome! She is always willing to share the lessons she has learned along the way and how she has acknowledged them. She leads with love and accepts that everyone has their issues to reconcile. She has been betrayed countless times and still finds a way to smile, laugh, welcome, and accept with such resilience. Anyone would love to learn how to do that because happiness is a choice… that comes with experience and wisdom gleaned throughout life.

Testimonials

I also feel that her fitness business is well-named because she is most certainly Fit2Motivate!

She has so much to offer, so I feel that leading retreats and mentoring (in addition to teaching boot camp, spin, and piano) is an awesome fit for her lifestyle and skill sets.

Janet Montemurro
Personal training client

DEDICATION

To the silent champions who graced my life with their unwavering presence, this book is dedicated with my deepest appreciation. In the whirlwind of the past year, Janessa, Janet, and Carrie-Anne emerged as my beacons of light.

Your unwavering support, your compassionate listening, and your unconditional acceptance have not only mended my spirit but have also reminded me of my worth and the abundant love that surrounds me. Your words of encouragement were lifelines in tumultuous waters, and your love

Cut The Anchor

was the anchor that steadied my soul. Your subtle acts of kindness were lifelines during turbulent times as I cut the anchor that was holding me down.

With this dedication, I hope to convey the depth of my appreciation and love.

Thank you, dear friends, from the very core of my being, for being my guiding stars, even when you didn't realize the profound impact you were making. I cherish each of you more than words can express.

With a thankful heart,

Kari Berridge

CONTENTS

Testimonials	iii
Dedication	vii
Introduction	1
Never Good Enough	7
The Invisible Monster	23
Deep Dark Hole	39
Hurt, Lies, Disbelief	53
Unraveling Toxic Relationships	73
Going It Alone	99
Thriving, Embracing, Empowering	121

Cut The Anchor

Insecurities, Freedoms, Headaches	139
Tragedy, Heartache, Growth	151
Resilient, Enduring, Transformative	171
The Big Secret	189
Living Life Authentically	205
About the Author	213
Speaker Bio	215
Acknowledgments	217
3 Offers with Call to Action	219
Book Review	221
Note From the Author	223
Cut the Anchor Book Club Questions	225

INTRODUCTION

Limiting self-beliefs, often referred to as negative self-talk or the inner critic, are the destructive thoughts and beliefs we hold about ourselves that undermine our confidence, self-worth, and overall well-being. These beliefs can have profound and far-reaching impacts on our lives, influencing various aspects of our mental, emotional, and even physical health. Here's a closer look at how limiting self-beliefs can affect us over a lifetime.

1. **Low self-esteem**: Constant, negative self-talk can erode our self-esteem and

self-confidence. We start doubting our abilities, accomplishments, and worth, which can hinder our personal and professional growth.
2. **Fear of failure**: Limiting beliefs can make us excessively fearful of failure, leading us to avoid taking risks and challenging ourselves. This fear of failure can hold us back from pursuing opportunities and reaching our full potential.
3. **Perfectionism:** Believing that we're not good enough can drive us towards perfectionism. We may feel the need to overcompensate for our perceived inadequacies, setting unrealistic standards.
4. **Imposter syndrome**: People with limiting self-beliefs often struggle with imposter syndrome, feeling like a fraud despite eternal evidence of competence.
5. **Social isolation**: Believing that we're not worthy of others' attention and affection can lead to social isolation. We may avoid forming connections out of fear of rejection or judgment.
6. **Depression and anxiety**: Persistent negative self-talk can contribute to the development of depression and anxiety disorders. The

Introduction

constant barrage of self-critical thoughts can wear down our mental resilience.

7. **Relationship issues**: Limiting beliefs can affect our relationships, as we might struggle to believe that someone could truly care for us. This can lead to trust issues, difficulty expressing emotions, and trouble forming healthy connections.
8. **Addiction and coping mechanisms**: Some individuals turn to addictive behaviors or substances to numb the pain of their negative self-beliefs. Addiction can be a way to escape from the harsh judgments they place on themselves.
9. **Physical health**: Chronic stress resulting from negative self-talk can have physical consequences, including a weakened immune system, sleep disturbances, and even cardiovascular issues.
10. **Career stagnation**: Believing we're not capable or deserving can lead to career stagnation. We may avoid pursuing promotions, new opportunities, or skill development, which can hinder professional growth.

Cut The Anchor

Breaking Down Limiting Self-Beliefs.

Shattering limiting self-beliefs requires conscious effort, self-awareness, and consistent work over time. Here are some strategies to overcome them:

1. **Self-compassion**: Treat yourself with the kindness and understanding you would offer a friend. Challenge negative self-talk with self-compassionate and supportive thoughts.
2. **Positive Affirmations**: Practice using positive affirmations to counteract negative beliefs. Repeat positive statements about yourself daily to reshape your self-perception.
3. **Cognitive behavioral therapy (CBT)**: CBT is a therapeutic approach that helps identify and challenge irrational thoughts and beliefs. Working with a therapist can be immensely beneficial.
4. **Mindfulness and meditation**: Mindfulness practices can help you observe your thoughts without judgment, giving you the space to choose healthier responses to negative self-talk.
5. **Seeking support**: Open up to trusted friends, family members, or mental health professionals about your struggles. Sometimes, an external perspective can provide valuable insights.

Introduction

6. **Setting realistic goals**: Setting achievable goals and celebrating small victories can gradually boost your self-confidence and challenge negative beliefs.
7. **Personal growth and learning**: Engage in activities that help you develop new skills and achieve personal growth. Each achievement can counteract the sense of inadequacy.
8. **Journalling**: Write down your thoughts and feelings. This practice can help you identify patterns of negative self-talk and work through them.

Remember that breaking down limiting self-beliefs is a journey that takes time and patience. The goal is not to eliminate all negative thoughts but to develop resilience and healthier responses to them. With consistent effort, you can rewrite the narrative you hold about yourself and lead a more fulfilling and empowered life.

The only limits you have are the limits you believe.

Wayne Dyer

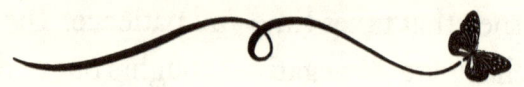

NEVER GOOD ENOUGH

Have you ever felt like you didn't fit in? Or that you were never good enough? Have you had self-limiting beliefs that have held you back from living your authentic life? Are you not living up to your true potential, and, if your answer is no, why not?

Perhaps you've encountered similar emotions within your own circle, be it among family, siblings, friends, or colleagues. The sentiment of never quite measuring

Cut The Anchor

up haunted my upbringing, accompanied by recurrent instances of feeling excluded. These emotions took root in my childhood, stemming from interactions with my immediate family, and persisted over the years through various friendships and even in my role as a parent. My upbringing revolved around a dynamic of favouritism; my dad displayed a clear preference for my brother, while my mom leaned toward my sister. Curiously, at some point, these roles seemed to reverse. Was this true for sure? I don't know, but as adults, my siblings and I would often engage in light-hearted banter, acknowledging, "Yeah, sorry Kar, we know you weren't the favourite." I would laugh, but I can't deny the sting of those words remained. Were there favourites in your family? And if so, where did you fit in?

I was a product of the generation where children were labeled. I received the label early on of the "responsible one." Looking at it now doesn't seem so bad but having that label as a young child put a lot of pressure on me to always be the good one. The one that never did anything wrong, never got into trouble, never skipped school, never smoked, drank, or did drugs. I never wanted to let my parents down, so I stayed the responsible one. And guess what I am as an adult? Yes, I am the responsible one.

Never Good Enough

Why couldn't I have been the rich one, the smart one, or the athletic one? Perception is everything. How we perceive things that are done or said to us can profoundly affect how we move forward in the world. Were there labels given to you and your siblings? What was the label given to you, and are you still living with that label? Did the label help or hinder you?

Words can hurt a person and stick with them for many years, if not their entire life. Words like "you're bossy," "you talk too much," "you're hard to get along with," and "you're abrupt." Instead of "you are a leader, a great communicator, straightforward, and focused." And how about the big ones like "You were one of the ugliest babies I had ever seen," "Don't get a fat bum or no one will love you," or, as you are about to walk down the aisle to marry your second husband, "So, do you think you can make this one work?" All of which were followed by "I was only joking; you take things too personally."

Our belief system serves as an imperceptible driving force underlying our actions. Alongside factors like our inherent personality, genetic composition, and established habits, our belief system stands as one of the most potent influences on every decision

Cut The Anchor

we undertake. It further extends its reach to encompass our modes of communication and our responses to life's unfolding events. Remarkably, an astonishing 95% of our belief framework about ourselves takes shape within specific periods of development: 50% between the formative years of zero to four, followed by 30% from four to eight, and a final 15% spanning from eight to eighteen years of age. Let that sink in for a moment. That can be a lot of negative beliefs about oneself before we even become an adult.

I have spent the better part of my life with negative, limiting self-beliefs that stemmed from things said to me as a child that weren't meant to harm but did just that. I tried to do things apart from my siblings so that I would stand out and get the attention I was desperately seeking. My brother and sister played baseball, so I chose soccer; my family was musical, but no one took piano lessons, so I did. My sister took lessons after I started, but, of course, she had the gift of playing by ear, which meant it came much easier to her than to me. Like most things, I had to work two or three times harder than my sister or brother. That is my perception anyway.

Never Good Enough

My sister got into trouble as a teenager, so I made sure I didn't just so I could stand out. It didn't work. The attention still seemed to be on her. Don't get me wrong; I loved my siblings, but I just wanted to feel as important or as good as they were.

So, I took a different approach to get noticed. I became an overachiever and a perfectionist. I started delivering papers at age ten, and by eleven I was babysitting for family members and then in time had regular babysitting jobs. By age sixteen I had three jobs: one at a store called Woolco, a great job at the University of Calgary cafeteria making great money, and babysitting. Then at seventeen, I had my first piano student, along with all the previous jobs mentioned. I worked hard, studied hard, and didn't get into trouble. I even graduated in two-and-a-half years doing the advanced route through high school. Again, I was trying to be seen and to feel like I was good enough just as I was. Sadly, I didn't feel it worked. What did you do in your family to get noticed? Or were you the lucky one that didn't have to work hard for it? But maybe that was just as bad; maybe being the favourite has its own set of problems.

Cut The Anchor

I was great with saving money, so when I was seventeen, I bought myself a brand-new car, a little Hyundai Pony. I worked hard and paid it off in six months. I was so excited, but I was met with "Well, if you hadn't bought other things, you could have paid it off in three months." A joke, perhaps, but I was devastated. I just longed to be told I made them proud. I was not very good at school and felt stupid throughout my entire twelve years in the school system. I recently found out I have ADHD, which makes a whole lot of sense looking back on my life now. I was a 70s student at best. I studied all the time, but I just couldn't get a grasp of the concepts taught. I remember coming home from school one day excited to show my mom my 80% mark on an English test. I was so pumped, only to be met with "Well, if you study more, you will do better next time." What? I knew that was the best I could do on an English or social paper. So, guess it was time to cheat, and cheat I did on my final, or I would never have passed. I was devastated and yet again felt like I was never good enough. I never met that bar that seemed so out of reach for me. Have you ever felt like that?

I remember standing in my parents' garage as an adult asking my mom why she liked the others better

Never Good Enough

than me, and she replied, "Because they are easier to get along with." I don't know what was going on in my mom's life at that point, but the comment stayed with me and probably always will. My mom is a very kind, caring, and quiet person, so she must have been dealing with something, or was it true that the other two were easier to get along with? Perhaps.

I felt I lived in my sister's shadow. She was prettier, smarter, taller, had all the guys, and was more athletic than me. I always tried to live up to her standard. The funny thing is I found out she always felt the same about me. It is interesting what you find out when you spend quality time talking with someone and asking the tough questions. Is this what happens in every family—living in your siblings' shadows? Or were you the one that your siblings tried to live up to?

My brother was good at anything he tried. I felt like he was better than me at everything, which he probably was. Oh, except when I was on top of my push-up game. I could do sixty full push-ups down to a fist. That I, for sure, was better at than him.

Being a very competitive person and driven by goals and results, I didn't like that he excelled while I struggled. My brother had been labeled the one "good at sports," but I remember one time after I finished an ultra-marathon, my brother said to me, "I guess dad backed the wrong horse." We had a good laugh.

I felt like all three of us siblings were very different when it came to communication with our parents. My brother would turtle. That's how I describe someone who doesn't like confrontation. He would avoid it at all costs. I called my sister the salesperson, which, funny enough, she ended up becoming. To me it meant someone who would say whatever they thought you wanted to hear just to appease you. I, on the other hand, called it like I saw it. If you were being an asshole, I called you one; if you were being mean or unfair, I told you so. I stuck up for myself and those I loved when things didn't appear to be fair. This didn't go over very well in my family, and, therefore, I didn't get along with my dad at all growing up. I felt I was always the butt of his jokes, but looking back on things, I think my siblings just handled it differently when it happened to them. They did admit on many occasions that I got it worse than they did, and again I feel it was because I didn't let up. I stood my ground until I finally just had to leave the room, or, as an adult,

Never Good Enough

I would leave and make the three-hour trip north back to my peaceful home. Sadly, this happened more often than I care to admit.

I remember driving down to my parents' home after I had kids of my own. I would get in the car and say to myself, "This time it's going to be better," and I would continue this phrase for the entire trip. But as my car inched closer and closer to my childhood home, I would start having the beginnings of a panic attack, knowing in my heart it wasn't going to be a better visit. It was going to be exactly how it always was. Which was full of stress and tension. I know this hurt my mom, and maybe in some small way she didn't want me to visit. Of course, she never said that to me, but I feel that my visiting put her in the middle, and that was never my intention. I just wanted to be loved and accepted for who I was, faults and all. Which I feel is what we all strive for. Isn't it?

Due to not receiving the essential attention I required, I was in search of acknowledgment and approval from others—a quest to ascertain whether they perceived what I perceived, or if it merely existed within my own thoughts.

Cut The Anchor

Over time, this tendency evolved into a recurring motif in my life: an unrelenting craving for acknowledgment and validation. I actively pursued it in various avenues, be it through friendships, relationships, marriages, and even, later, with my grown children. I can only imagine how draining this must have been for those around me. I now see that validation must come from within and not from an outside source.

My self-esteem was alarmingly low, leaving me with an overwhelming craving for attention, support, and affection. As time passed, a handful of my close friends began to question, "Does your dad always communicate with you that way?" Strangely, I would often fail to notice because I had grown so accustomed to it over the years. Even my children observed this behavior as they grew older. Yet, there seemed to be a lack of active supporters, leaving me with a persistent sensation of isolation on my metaphorical island.

My daughter stuck up for me one time when she was about fifteen, which unfortunately ended with my sister and me not talking for a year. My sister didn't like the way my daughter talked to my dad, but I taught my kids to stick up for the ones we

Never Good Enough

love. And because this incident took place in my home, my daughter felt it was inappropriate for my dad to be putting me down, especially because I wasn't there to defend myself. I was on the way to the airport to drop off my brother.

I had one friend stick up for me about eight years ago, which was the first time anyone other than my daughter had ever done that for me. I remember crying when she told me that she spent two hours the previous night talking to my dad regarding the hurtful way in which he had spoken to me. She explained to him that girls just want to be loved and adored by their fathers. This was one of those times when I had left the room and gone downstairs to bed when the picking on me started. I knew my girlfriend could hold her own, and, apparently, she did. I think that was a turning point for me. I finally knew that it wasn't in my head and that the constant picking on was real. I used to say, "Okay, the knife is bloody enough," referring to someone sticking a knife into someone and continually twisting it until it couldn't be twisted anymore.

But then I was on to the next question, which was why?

Why was I the butt of the jokes, why didn't he like me, why did he like my siblings better than me? After years of therapy, journalling, reading, and self-development courses, I realized that my dad just likes to have an audience because when it is just him and I, we have some great conversations. He likes to get the laughs any way he can, and if that means I am the butt of the jokes, so be it. I have also realized that my dad and I are very much the same person in many ways. And perhaps that is where the friction stemmed from. When we see something in others that we don't like within ourselves, it tends to gnaw at us. But I did take on a lot of his great qualities, from handling money well to being a leader, being the planner of functions, loving fitness, taking an authentic interest in others, and finding out their story because we all have one. I now know after years of self-work that my dad does love me; he is proud of me, even though I haven't heard those words directly from him; and he thinks I have done a great job raising my kids as a single mom—that one he did tell me. And that is good enough for me.

Not only was I fighting for a place within my family and dealing with the constant digs, but I also battled teasing in other areas of my life. It

Never Good Enough

started in elementary school, where I was teased relentlessly by the other students because I twitched my nose and blinked my eyes a lot. It turns out I have Tourette syndrome and have had it since the age of five. I just didn't know it back then.

I wasn't officially diagnosed until the age of twenty-seven, which is a long time to have something and not know what it is or why you do the things you do. I grew up thinking there was something seriously wrong with me. When I was married the second time, I was watching Oprah one day, and it was on the topic of Tourette syndrome, which I had never heard of to that point. I was mesmerized by the information I was hearing. Everything they were saying was exactly like me, so I called my mom right away and told her I think Dad and I have Tourette's. Her response floored me. She said, "Yes, I know." What did she mean, she knew? Why was I never told? What possible reason would there be to not tell your child what they had? It would have made things a lot easier knowing that I wasn't crazy like I thought I was all those years. Here all I had was Tourette's, which I say in jest because having Tourette's is not fun at all. As my son said when he was eight years old, "I would rather have a pitbull bite my face off, chew it up, and spit it out than have

Cut The Anchor

Tourette's." This broke my heart, but I understood how he felt. One memory I have of when I was younger is that I would be in the back seat of my parents' car saying to myself, "Don't twitch, don't twitch." I was trying to make it from one light post to another without twitching, which I was never able to do. Then I would beat myself up by saying, "I'm a loser. What is wrong with me?"

I assumed the role of a child who advocated for both myself and those who were powerless. This character, while I believed it to be morally correct, was often misconstrued by many as disruptive behavior. My tendency for outspokenness, which might have been deemed disrespectful during my childhood, is something I hold in high regard. I take pride in my actions.

Throughout my school years, I consistently stood up for those who were subject to bullying and mistreatment, a trait that endures in me to this day. It's possible that I embraced this stance due to the absence of anyone defending me during my own experiences. Were you bullied in school? Were you the one who bullied? And if so, was it because you were hurting inside, or maybe you were being bullied at home in some way?

Never Good Enough

My feelings of not being good enough continued to follow me up until recently. It affected every relationship I had from friendships to boyfriends, husbands, siblings, teachers, my parents, and even my children. I was constantly looking for outside validation because inside I never felt good enough, smart enough, or worthy enough. Through this last year of transformation, I have now come to the realization I was always good enough and that my parents have always loved me and wanted the best for me. They showed their love in a different way than I needed, and I don't fault them for that. I don't blame them anymore; I've cut the chains of anger and resentment and have replaced them with love and compassion. I now realize they did the absolute best with the tools they had at the time.

The journey of self-discovery, which I call "my Kari journey" started in my thirties, with this last year being immersed in breaking down the self-limiting beliefs that I absorbed as a child. This tough but exciting journey has brought me to a place of loving myself, all of me, the good and the bad, and realizing my self-worth comes from within and I don't need outside validation. Seeking outside validation has held me back from living up to my true potential. I am a strong, independent, loving,

Cut The Anchor

caring, intelligent, and authentic woman. I am proud of who I have become. I am forward-moving and will continue to break through any limiting beliefs that come up throughout my life until this incredible journey comes to an end. If you feel like you are ready to bust through those limiting self-beliefs that have been holding you back, I am here to tell you it is possible.

*It's not what you say out loud that determines your life.
It's what you whisper to yourself that has the most power!*

Robert T. Kiyosaki

THE INVISIBLE MONSTER

Do you know anyone who is living with or has recovered from an eating disorder? Or perhaps it is you? Living with an eating disorder is extremely tough, and for some it can be deadly.

I never knew much about eating disorders until I was living with one. I was very thin growing up and got teased by kids in school for how skinny I was. I don't recall being a big eater as I preferred to eat small amounts all day long. I wasn't trying to be thin; however, that all changed when I was sixteen. That summer, I got a job working away from home. Because I didn't have a lot of money to spend on food, I ended up eating a lot of burgers and fries. I don't remember thinking I had gained weight, but upon returning home I was informed by friends and family just how "fat" I had gotten over the summer. I was devastated. Yet another thing to add to my list of ways I wasn't "good enough." This is what happens when you have no self-esteem: you absorb any negative words thrown at you. Rather than ignoring the hurtful words, you take them in, swirl them around in your head, and make them far worse than how they were originally meant.

At age sixteen I started going to Weight Watchers, which started the rollercoaster of my weight obsession. At first, I wanted to lose those ten pounds everyone talks about. I started working out a couple hours every night in my parents' basement. I followed the Weight Watchers plan and ate less than the plan suggested. I needed to shed those ten unwanted pounds. I would work out and then go straight to bed. This way I wouldn't feel the urge to eat. At this point, I had exercise-induced anorexia, but I was unaware of it at the time. Anorexia athletica is an eating disorder characterized by

The Invisible Monster

excessive and compulsive exercising. I started weighing myself every day, which I don't recall doing before that summer. I remember feeling proud of myself if I didn't eat and angry at myself when I did. This continued for six months. Then, after shedding the first ten pounds, I thought, what about another ten? Which I successfully lost as well.

I moved out of my parent's home a couple of weeks after I turned eighteen and took the three-hour journey north to Edmonton, where I still reside. I couldn't afford to eat the nutritional food you find around the perimeter of the grocery store. So, I stuck to the middle section, where all the less nutritional, cheaper food sits. Fruits and vegetables were not in my budget, but Ichiban soup, Kraft dinner, and potato chips were affordable.

Not long after I arrived, I got a job at a restaurant that was attached to a country bar, which I frequented often. After we all got off shift, we sat around eating a huge plate of nachos with all the fixings: sour cream, loads of cheese, you name it. This became my main meal of the day because it was free. We also got drinks for cheap since we worked there. Singapore slings were my go-to. Or should I say red, colorful, sugary alcohol was my drink of

Cut The Anchor

choice! I would go on dates just so I could eat a healthy meal. That sounds horrible, but it was my only option since I couldn't afford healthy groceries. So that ten pounds I lost at age sixteen came back, times four. My boyfriend at the time, who became my first husband, used to make fun of me along with his best friend. Saying "MOOOOO" every time I walked into the room. The creative name they gave my calves was "heifers." Of course, it hurt my feelings, but ultimately what it did was spur me on to lose that initial ten pounds again, which turned into another ten, and then I just kept going. I started walking to and from work, which was about fifty minutes each way, up and down steep hills. Once I got to the office building, I would then walk up seventeen flights of stairs to my office. I did this every day just to lose weight, and then I was hooked. Ten pounds turned to another ten to another until I reached a low of ninety-eight pounds. This was my weight on the day of my first wedding at age twenty-one.

I remember years later, when my daughter was around twenty, she wanted to try my wedding dress on, and it didn't fit her, and she was a normal, healthy weight. So, when my son walked in, we got him to try it on, just for fun. He was almost fifteen,

The Invisible Monster

and it fit him. I can't remember how I felt about this because I was still suffering from anorexia at the time. But looking back on it, I feel very sad to know that I was that thin, and I wonder what my kids must have thought trying on that dress.

According to the National Initiative Eating Disorders Association, the statistics concerning eating disorders are nothing short of alarming. In Canada alone, the numbers reveal that approximately one million individuals have been diagnosed with various forms of eating disorders, including anorexia nervosa, bulimia nervosa, binge eating disorder, and avoidant restrictive food intake disorder. Eating disorders constitute a grave, yet treatable, category of mental illness that can impact individuals regardless of their gender, age, racial or ethnic background, sexual orientation, or socioeconomic status. Tragically, a considerable number of individuals suffering from these disorders go undiagnosed, resulting in significant distress for both them and their families. The consequences of untreated eating disorders bear a resemblance to those of depression and anxiety, leading to debilitating effects on both physical and mental well-being that can be compared to the challenges posed by psychosis and schizophrenia. While

Cut The Anchor

it is widely acknowledged that mental illnesses contribute significantly to premature mortality in Canada, the lesser-known truth is that eating disorders possess the highest overall mortality rate within the realm of mental illnesses, with estimates ranging between 10-15%. Shockingly, suicide stands as the second leading cause of death—only trailing behind cardiac disease—among those struggling with an eating disorder. It's disheartening to acknowledge that around 20% of individuals with anorexia and 25-35% of those with bulimia might attempt suicide during their lifetime. Among females aged fifteen to twenty-four, the mortality rate linked to anorexia surpasses that of ALL other causes of death combined by a staggering twelve-fold. These statistics undeniably serve as a wake-up call, urging us to shed more light on the subject and promote open discussions about this critical issue.

From my experiencing anorexia firsthand for a better part of my life, this is what I have learned about the disease. I was in control of what I ate or didn't eat, and for the first time in my life, I had control over something when it came to myself. I never had any control growing up. None of my siblings did. What you do or don't put in your mouth, however, is one of the only things you truly

The Invisible Monster

have control over—until you don't! It's a sickness that controls the mind. It is a silent killer and so hard to explain to others.

In my experience, anorexia is like walking a very fine line. I was in control of what I did or didn't eat, and I weighed myself every day, sometimes three or four times. If I gained a pound or even a few ounces, to be honest, I just wouldn't eat the next day. I felt I had "won" if I went to bed hungry, and I had "lost" if I gave in and ate when the hunger pains presented themselves. I would beat myself up with horrible negative self-talk when I would give in and eat something I shouldn't. It was such a mind fuck. But I still felt I was in control. Then, all of a sudden—or at least that is how it felt for my eating-disordered brain—the disease now controlled me. It felt like a snap of the finger and there I was—anorexic! I am not sure if all eating disorders are like this, but this was my experience. The topic of food was like a monster living inside my head. "Eat just enough but not too much." "Don't eat that or you will get fat, and no one will like you." "Be strong—don't put that in your mouth." "You ate too much—you are weak." "You have hunger pains—good, that means you won today." "You are going to bed full—try to do better tomorrow." The voices just never stopped.

Cut The Anchor

Have you ever experienced this? If so, I completely understand. If not, you are very lucky.

When I became pregnant the first time, I gained eighteen pounds, just enough to produce a healthy seven-and-a-half-pound baby girl. Within a week I was back in the gym (not okayed by my doctor) and back in my size-three jeans. I was so proud of myself. Read that again. I was so proud of myself. That sounds crazy, doesn't it? But it was my reality. Being pregnant while suffering from anorexia messes with the mind—being "fat" for nine months was awful. I hated being pregnant! I am not sure what led me to get help, but I started seeing a specialist that dealt with eating disorders. But because I was so messed up, I was defiant, aggressive, had a chip on my shoulder, always looking for a fight, and didn't feel I was getting the help from him that I needed. Looking back now, I am sure it was just an excuse to stay thin. I quit seeing him and tried to deal with it on my own for the next fifteen years. I didn't do too well at that. I was scared to gain weight. Even one pound would send me into a tailspin. I continued to weigh myself every day, which I still do. This is not a good thing for someone with an eating disorder. Whether I am a recovered anorexic or still suffering. I know

The Invisible Monster

some people who have completely overcome an eating disorder, but, unfortunately for me, I still have a hard time with my weight.

When I got married the second time, I was still very thin. About a year later, we found out we were pregnant with twins. Oh no, here we go again. I gained about forty pounds this time—again, I hated being pregnant—I felt like a massive whale. I loved being a mom; I just didn't like the pregnancy part. It took longer to lose the weight this time because of the amount I gained. Even though I was tired And looking after three kids, I still managed to fit Jane Fonda workouts in. I also found a place to take fitness classes at the old jail gym where I could take my boys with me while my daughter was in school. And within four to five months, I was back to my pre-pregnancy weight. I don't remember much about my weight during the rest of the marriage, just that I was thin.

After this marriage ended, my anorexia got worse. My diet consisted of three to four cans of Coke, four arrowroot baby cookies, an apple, and one slice of peanut butter toast each day. I don't drink coffee, so I think the Coke just gave me that caffeine I needed to get through the day since I had no energy from

Cut The Anchor

not eating. Then it switched to just Diet Coke (oh, so much better than Coke—insert eye roll) and pretzels. That was pretty much all I ate. I asked a specialist why I would eat pretzels and drink Coke if I had an eating disorder. Her answer was this: anorexia takes on different forms: some eat very little and then throw up, some eat very little and don't make themselves throw up, and I fell into the latter. I never threw up, but I would eat very little. So, my anorexic brain told me it was okay to just have Coke and pretzels because if that was all I was eating I wouldn't gain weight. I do not ever remember thinking about healthy foods that I should be consuming; it was just all about the small quantity of food I put in my body. Therefore, Coke and pretzels are what I lived on for years.

I was so scared to gain weight—if I did splurge one day and have a bit more to eat, I would then not eat for a few days. This went on for the next fifteen years. Not only was I eating horribly, but I also never drank water until I was in my thirties, which sounds crazy to me now, since today I won't leave the house without my bag of filtrated Kangen water. I drink it every day, all day long. Water is so important for our health!

The Invisible Monster

If you have ever watched a movie with an anorexic person in it, they almost always show them looking in a full-length mirror, and to them, they see a fat person staring back while the audience sees a skeleton in the mirror. I can say from experience that is exactly what happened to me. I truly did not see that I was extremely thin. I still don't feel thin, even to this day. Unless I am looking at photos or a video of myself, I don't see myself as being overly thin.

Just the other day, I was waiting for my car to be fixed, and a lady who had been in my spin class before COVID was picking up her car. We started talking, and the first thing she said was "Are you sick? You are very thin." I was a little taken aback because, even though I know I am on the thinner side, I still don't think it's extreme.

Food has always been an issue—it isn't an enjoyable thing for me; it is just fuel for my body at this point. But at least I now understand the importance of eating nutritional food for energy, brain function, and healthy skin, teeth, and eyes. It supports muscles, boosts immunity, strengthens bones, lowers the risk of heart disease, cancers, and much more.

Cut The Anchor

Food was always an ordeal in my extended family; they would make comments if you were too thin or too fat and about what was on your plate—too much or not enough. It seemed never-ending. I thought all families were like that until I went to my second husband's family reunion and food never got brought up once. I said to him, "No one talks about food here," and he said, "What are you talking about?" I was just so shocked. Food was, and still is to some degree, a big deal with my family. It did a lot of damage to my mental state.

When I was in my thirties, I took up bodybuilding and competed four times. I was assured by my trainers they would help me transition to a normal weight again after the competition as I had told them ahead of time that I had been anorexic to this point. This was not the case, however, and I was left to deal with it on my own. I gained forty-five pounds within three weeks after the competition, and I went into a depression. I started doing cardio for two to three hours a day to get the weight off. It took me three years to get down to 128 pounds, where I stayed for a while, but I still felt fat. I tried many different diets, which is the worst thing an anorexic can do. I knew I needed to be careful, so I didn't go back to the low weight I was previously, and I

The Invisible Monster

knew the warning signs. As I mentioned earlier, I never threw up having anorexia; I just didn't eat for days if I felt fat. Then I started taking water pills, a trick I learned from the body-building world. If I had too much sodium intake and felt puffy, I would take a water pill. Brilliant—or so I thought at the time. This is not good for our bodies. If you take a thiazide diuretic, your potassium level can drop too low, which can cause life-threatening problems with your heartbeat. It can cause worsening kidney function and light-headedness or dizziness as a result of being dehydrated.

If someone commented, even if unintentional, about my body, I wouldn't eat for days. Even the comment "It's nice to see you have put on a bit of weight" would give me a reason not to eat until I lost the few pounds I had gained. To someone who has never suffered from an eating disorder, they may not understand how those simple words could mean so much more than they were meant to. We do need to be careful with the words we choose to use with others. I know the word "fat" has a negative connotation, but I use the word because that is how I felt for fifteen years. I don't like using that word; however, it unfortunately is the perception of an anorexic.

Cut The Anchor

I am still thin to this day. I would say I am a recovered anorexic standing on the thin line between anorexia and a healthy weight. The digestive issues I have been dealing with for the last six years haven't helped with my issues with weight. And because of being ill at this point in my life, food continues to occupy my thoughts, just in a different way now. There's not a lot I can eat due to my health issues, but perhaps it all stems from being anorexic for so long, not having proper nutrition, and the ongoing stress of life. I am still in the process of figuring this out.

What I know from experience is eating disorders can be all-consuming, they can create havoc on our bodies, our minds, and our lives. My hope for myself and others is to break through the barriers of self-doubt surrounding weight. We are all loveable, no matter what our size is. We have so many things to offer the world, and what we weigh has no bearing on our self-worth. I know I can help others to overcome this even as I continue to work through it myself. I have been on this journey for the last forty years and have a lot to offer others working through it themselves. We shouldn't have to go through it alone.

The Invisible Monster

*Courage does not always roar.
Sometimes courage is the quiet voice
At the end of the day saying,
"I will try again tomorrow."*

Mary Anne Radmacher

DEEP DARK HOLE

Have you ever suffered from depression? Postpartum depression? Or know someone who has?

Well, not only was I suffering from anorexia as a young woman, but I was also battling depression that started as undiagnosed postpartum depression.

According to Postpartum Depression.org, postpartum depression is a mood disorder that can affect women following childbirth. Mothers struggling with this condition often find themselves dealing with symptoms that include feelings of hopelessness and emptiness, recurring and unexplained bouts of tears, changes in eating patterns, heightened anxiety, and a range of anger expressions extending from irritability to intense rage. Additional signs of postpartum include diminished interest in activities that were once enjoyed. It is essential to recognize that all pregnant women are susceptible to postpartum depression, regardless of age, race, ethnicity, or economic standing. However, the likelihood of its onset increases if you have a personal history of depression or if someone within your family has experienced it before. This was true in my case.

From my understanding, PPD is linked to chemical imbalances in the brain that can lead to erratic behavior and mood fluctuations. These changes, combined with the lack of sleep frequently experienced by new mothers, can intensify the symptoms of PPD.

Effective treatment typically involves a combination of talk therapy and medication. If PPD is untreated it has the potential to persist for extended periods, even years, like in my case. PPD can show up anywhere from a few days after birth to a year. This gap between childbirth and the onset of symptoms can lead affected individuals to misunderstand their condition, which again is what happened to me.

According to the Mayo Clinic, general depression is a mood disorder that causes a persistent feeling of sadness and loss of interest. It affects how you feel, think, and behave and can lead to a variety of emotional and physical problems. You may have trouble doing normal day-to-day activities, and sometimes you may feel as if life isn't worth living. More than just a bout of the blues, depression isn't a weakness, and you can't simply "snap out of it" as some may think. Depression may require long-term treatment.

Allow me to share my personal journey through depression.

At age twenty, I had a newborn, was suffering from anorexia, had no family around to help, was with a man who was emotionally abusive, and did not have many friends. And I was now trying to figure out why I was so sad all the time. I would lie on my couch holding my daughter for hours at a time. I would muster up the energy to take her for a walk in her stroller, but other than that I didn't do much other than cry and take care of her. I did not receive much help or support from her dad, which made it hard for me. I remember making a chart and putting it on the fridge door so he would do his part in changing her diapers. I believe it lasted one day before he took it down and threw it in the garbage. I was also on my own emotionally, as it appeared to me that he wasn't interested in the domestic part of a relationship or raising a child. His interests were hockey, drinking beer, and cheating on me, in no particular order.

However, when my daughter was ten months old, her dad and I made the poor choice to get married. There is no blame here; however, had someone told me I didn't have to get married I absolutely would not have. We divorced soon after due to the fact he got another woman pregnant four months after our wedding. I'll talk about it more in a subsequent chapter.

So now, I was an anorexic twenty-one-year-old single mom to a fourteen-month-old, without a job, no family close by, and still not many friends. Plus, I was suffering from postpartum depression, which I did not know I had. Life was extremely hard at this point. I didn't even tell my parents I was divorced because I was embarrassed; I didn't want to have to admit I failed at something yet again.

Deep Dark Hole

It was this black cloud I talked about that kept following me around. Or so I thought at the time. What I came to learn later is this: what you put out there is what comes back. If you manifest a black cloud following you around, that is exactly what will happen. If you manifest great things happening to you, that is exactly what will happen. I, however, didn't learn this until I was in my thirties.

The only reason I told my parents about the divorce was because six months after we split up, they were coming to visit, and I needed to inform them of my new address. Otherwise, who knows when I would have gotten around to telling them? I used to keep a lot inside and not tell anyone anything about my life, and I believe looking back it was because I didn't feel that important. I wondered why anyone cared about what I did or didn't do or how I felt about things. I was also making so many poor choices at that point in my life that I didn't want anyone to know anything about me. It was safer that way. By doing this there were no expectations from others, only the ones I put on myself. Which I grew to learn were far tougher expectations than anyone else could ever have put on me. So, I stayed guarded and lived my life that way for a very long time. It is a very lonely way to live.

Cut The Anchor

I had talked to my general physician many times about how sad I was, but she just wasn't hearing me. She kept telling me I was fine and that all moms get a bit sad after having a baby. I knew I wasn't okay, so I kept advocating for myself until finally, after more than a year of asking, she gave me a referral to a psychologist who then sent me to a psychiatrist. By this point, my daughter was around two years old. He put me on medication for my depression, which by now had changed from postpartum depression to general depression, and suggested I be part of this cognitive therapy test group being run at the University of Alberta Hospital. I remember thinking, what did I have to lose? It was quite an eye-opening experience for me because there were people from every walk of life in that group, all suffering from depression. There was a judge, an older woman, a burn victim, and men and women of all ages. Here I thought it was just me and that I was being punished for something I had done. But no, it was something I had no control over. The group met twice a week for four hours each time and lasted for six months. There was always homework to do, and I remember one of our first assignments was to write out all the things we liked about ourselves. It couldn't be "I am a good mom" or "I keep a clean home"; the list

Deep Dark Hole

had to be traits or qualities about ourselves that we liked. I worked and worked on that list, and when I came back to the group the following week my paper was completely empty. There was not one thing I liked about myself. In fact, I hated myself. Have you ever felt this way?

I never missed a class, and I thought I was doing much better after it, as I had learned a lot of thinking techniques that I still use to this day. For example, instead of saying I have ugly hair, switch it to I am having a bad hair day. Or, instead of saying I am a shitty mom, say I handled a parenting situation poorly. It is the way we see, think, and say things that make a difference.

I thought I was doing much better. However, depression doesn't work that way. About two months after the course ended, when my daughter was around two and a half, my friend (at that point he was my only friend) had taken my daughter to her swim lesson so I could have a bit of alone time. I used it very wisely: I went up to my room, took the bottle of my antidepressants, and swallowed them all.

I felt so alone, discouraged, sad, and overwhelmingly full of dread. I was a very lost soul at this point in my life. I felt I was a burden to the few who loved me and believed it would be better for all if I just weren't here anymore. I never wanted to commit suicide to hurt anyone; it wasn't out of being selfish like a lot of people believe about suicides. It's not a selfish act. It is a desperate one. For me, it was truly out of a place of feeling nothing. I explained it like a big dark black hole that I just couldn't climb out of. I had been down for so long and had no self-confidence whatsoever. I just wanted the suffering to end.

Luckily my friend found me when he got back with my daughter, and he rushed me to the hospital to get my stomach pumped. I don't remember much about the after-effects as I have a great ability to shove things deep down as if they never happened. Little pieces come to the surface at times but not often. It is how I have protected myself for the better part of my life. "Build that big wall around the heart and don't let anyone in" seemed to be my motto. Most days were dark, and I just couldn't find any shimmer of light.

I look back at pictures of myself during those years of depression and I see a lonely, sad, broken look in my eyes. Even when I was laughing or smiling, I

Deep Dark Hole

still looked so sad. The eyes truly are the window to a person's soul. I faked being happy for the better part of my life, and I put on a great act so no one would know that deep down I was so very lost. I had some great, amazing times but at the core, I felt lonely, hurt, angry, tired, confused, unlovable, broken, and unworthy, and I had no self-love.

I would go on antidepressants, and when I was feeling good, I would think I didn't need pills anymore and I would go off, only to feel worse than before. I finally understood after the third time that I had to wean off and not go off cold turkey. I had been told this earlier by my doctor, but I always seemed to think I knew more than others did at that time in my life. I battled for the next thirteen years until finally in my thirties I was able to go off the antidepressants for good, or so I thought. When I went through perimenopause I went back on them, as I started getting panic attacks during this time and was completely out of sorts. Then I was off them only to return to them again when my sister passed away and I was at an all-time low.

There is absolutely nothing wrong with being on antidepressants, and at times in most people's lives, they may need them. Taking medication for

Cut The Anchor

your depression can help you get your life back to normal. I have found, though, that the medication just gets you out of that black hole. But some kind of therapy, like cognitive behavioral therapy (CBT), interpersonal therapy, or supportive therapy, is also needed. The more we talk about our feelings, or journal or read about depression and ways to feel better, the better chance we have of becoming happier and being able to cope with those hard times in our lives. We all handle things differently, and we all have challenging times in our lives. No one is immune to this—it's how we handle things that change from person to person. If you are feeling depressed, please seek help. Talk to a friend or your doctor, or find a coach like me to help you through those feelings of despair. There is help out there for you. Please know you aren't alone; people love you and truly want to see you happy.

Depression has been a recurring presence in my family's history, and it saddens me to see that many of my relatives still struggle with this illness. While the conversation around mental health has evolved considerably over the years, there remains a reluctance among some to openly discuss it. Reflecting on my own journey, I recall a time when tears made me uncomfortable, and I associated them with weakness. Perhaps this stemmed from my perception of my parents' roles in my life: my dad, always stoic, was the model of strength, while my mom, who frequently shed tears, was seen as more vulnerable.

However, as I have grown over the past decade, my perspective on expressing emotions has shifted significantly. Witnessing individuals I know openly acknowledge their struggles with mental health, I've come to admire their strength in doing so. It prompted me to question why I couldn't do the same. Crying, which once made me uneasy, became a cathartic release for me, and in 2018, I found myself finally allowing those emotions to flow freely. They haven't stopped since.

According to the Canadian Mental Health Association, the prevalence of mental illness in Canada is indeed staggering, casting a shadow on a significant portion of the population. In any given year, approximately one in three Canadians struggle with a mental health condition. By the time individuals reach forty years of age, this ratio increases to one in every two, highlighting the widespread impact of mental health issues. Young people, particularly those aged fifteen to twenty-four, confront a higher likelihood of experiencing mental illnesses and substance use disorders than any other age group. Tragically, the somber reality of suicide claims around 4,000 Canadian lives annually, averaging nearly eleven suicides per day. This alarming statistic underscores the urgency of addressing mental health concerns across all demographics and backgrounds.

However, a substantial stigma surrounding mental illness continues to linger, inhibiting open conversations and necessary support. This stigma was evident in a 2019 survey of working Canadians, revealing that 75% of respondents would be hesitant or unwilling to disclose a mental illness to employers or colleagues. This reluctance stemmed from fears of being treated differently, judged, and facing negative consequences, including potential job loss. Remarkably, the same survey highlighted a heartening contradiction: 76% of respondents expressed complete comfort and support for colleagues dealing with mental illness. This juxtaposition underscores the compassion and empathy that often lie beneath the surface, suggesting that a personal understanding of mental health struggles fosters a more compassionate and supportive outlook.

Deep Dark Hole

My own experience mirrors this dichotomy—wishing to be open about mental health but being met with reservations due to real concerns about potential consequences. Sharing your own journey can inspire understanding and facilitate destigmatization. The more individuals speak openly about mental health, the closer we come to erasing the barriers that prevent individuals from seeking help, advocating for change, and creating a society that is genuinely inclusive and supportive of those facing mental health challenges.

Raising three children while suffering from depression was extremely hard, and I wish now that I would have talked about it more with them when they were growing up. I was too busy trying to be the perfect mom, and I didn't want my kids to view me in a poor light. Hindsight is everything. I wish that I had been more open and authentic about what I was going through. But being a single mom and trying to be everything to everyone was all I was thinking about at the time. I was just trying to survive.

I was not sure why I was put on this great place we call Earth. However, I had a strong desire to figure out what my purpose was. I knew that everything

Cut The Anchor

I had faced up to this point must have something to do with why I was here. I just didn't figure it out until I was in my thirties when the real work on myself began.

If you or someone you know is suffering from PPD or any form of depression, please know that you are not alone. There is help out there for you, and there are people that love you. Even if you can't see it, they are there.

> *There are wounds that never*
> *show on the body*
> *that are deeper and more hurtful*
> *than anything that bleeds.*
>
> **Laurell K. Hamilton**

HURT, LIES, DISBELIEF

Have you ever been cheated on? Have you ever done the cheating, whether emotionally or physically? Have you lied to those you love? Sadly, I have done all of these in the past.

According to a poll conducted by Mainstreet Research for Postmedia News after the breach of Ashley Madison's data, 22% of Canadians have seriously considered cheating on their partner. 10% of Canadians admit to having cheated on their significant other, with more men than women admitting to this behavior. 13% of males and 8% of females admitted to infidelity, and 23% of men and 20% of women have seriously considered committing the act. These transgressions can manifest as either physical or emotional infidelities, both of which have the potential to shatter relationships. Ironically, in some cases, these crises can lead to a stronger bond between partners. This was not the case in my first marriage, as it was already pretty shitty to begin with.

After around thirty-five infidelities, with approximately six women that I know of (it could be much higher), he finally got caught by getting the last one pregnant. I got the nerve up and told him to leave. Many ask how I know it was around thirty-five times. Well, I figured it out after a while. The only time I ever got roses was after he had cheated. So, I started adding up the times I received a dozen roses, and it totaled around thirty-five. Some may say that maybe he bought me roses just because. I can pretty much guarantee that wasn't the case with this man.

Some may ask, why did you stay so long when you knew he was cheating on you? Others asked why I married him. These are great questions, but they

Hurt, Lies, Disbelief

can be interpreted as a blaming question when asked in this manner. Blaming the person who remains in a relationship where their partner engages in infidelity, instead of holding the unfaithful partner responsible for damaging the trust in the relationship, is a misguided perspective. A better way perhaps to ask that question would be "How are you doing with everything that is happening?" Or just say, "I am sorry this has happened, and I want you to know I am here for you if you need anything." Those questions or statements stay neutral, at the same time still being there for the person you care about.

But to answer the question, there were a few reasons I stayed, and most had to do with my limiting self-beliefs. I stayed because I had no self-esteem or self-worth, I didn't think highly of myself and therefore thought he was as good as I deserved. Because that is what he told me on many occasions. I had to work so hard to get the love I wanted growing up that it seemed natural for me to have to fight for his attention and affection. It was all I knew at that point in my life.

A few of his infidelities stand out to me. He came home a few times too many with his lunch uneaten, and when I asked about it, he said, "Well, I was at so and so's." (I really couldn't tell you her name as I have blocked it out.) But it was his ex-girlfriend. I was instantly upset—extremely jealous—hmm, I wonder why? I asked him why he had been there, and he gave me a story about needing to change her tires. Yes, "I bet you changed her tires" is all I could say. He tried to deny it but, in the end, the truth came out, and his response was "Well, fat girls like to fuck too, you know." That response will never leave me. He didn't think he had done anything wrong; this is what baffled me by his response.

Another one comes to mind: I was at EXPO in Vancouver while he was playing in the Oilmen's Hockey tournament, which occurred every May in Edmonton. I had been told the previous two years that the wives or girlfriends weren't allowed to attend any functions; it was just for the players. Naïve little Kari believed this. Boy, was I naïve back then. His best friend, however, was dating my girlfriend at the time. I got a call from her asking why I wasn't at the banquet. I asked what banquet she was referring to and told her he said no women were allowed. She said, "Well, he lied to you. I just saw him get off the elevator with another woman and head to his hotel room with her." I was

Hurt, Lies, Disbelief

devastated, but looking back I am not sure why as I knew he had done it before. Of course, when I got home and confronted him, he lied yet again and said my friend had made it all up. I honestly don't remember what I did or said, but, clearly, I stayed with him. Again, I felt unworthy.

Another one that comes to mind transpired between him and his female best friend. I was working two jobs at the time, a full-time job and a part-time one as well. I took that part-time job so I could pay off that Hyundai Pony I had bought right before moving to Edmonton. I was at my second job when I called home, and he didn't answer. I tried a couple more times, and still no answer. It was my first night at the part-time job, and I was excited to tell him about it. When he finally answered on the fourth try, he said he had been out for dinner. I inquired who he had gone with, and he quickly replied just himself. Which for some isn't a red flag, but this was out of character for him. He would never have gone for dinner by himself. I couldn't get home quick enough that night to find out the truth, but when I got there, he had already left for hockey, so I did something I had never done before. I wasn't raised by parents who looked through our things; they trusted us until we proved them wrong.

Cut The Anchor

Snooping, reading others' things, going through diaries, and listening in on phone calls was just not something I was used to. However, I did just that because that gut feeling that was nagging at me needed to be addressed. And sure enough, there it was! A receipt in his coat pocket, a dinner for two. Busted! I remember calling someone close to me and telling them I was so upset I just wanted to take a baseball bat and smash the one thing he truly loved, which was his T.V. The trusted person on the other end said, "Well, maybe there is a reason. Just go talk to him." Okay, so, let me get this correct: there could be a *good* reason why someone cheats on someone they supposedly love? I wasn't aware this could be a thing. Again, insert eye roll here. However, I got into my car and drove fifty minutes across town in a whiteout blizzard so I could ask him what his good reason for cheating on me was, yet again. When I walked into the rink, his best friend was walking out of the dressing room. He saw me, and I asked, "Where is he?"

"The dressing room," he replied.

"Please go get him," I said. Who am I kidding, there was no "please." It was more of a command: "GO GET HIM." He was surprised to see me

Hurt, Lies, Disbelief

and caught off guard when I called him out on yet another lie. And because of this, he admitted to this affair. And again, I stayed with him.

The infidelity that ended it all, however, was with the woman he got pregnant. We had changed insurance companies, which meant we had to go in to sign papers. So off we went to the downtown office. Once in the room, I had an uneasy feeling about the female insurance agent and my husband. It wasn't anything they said or did; it was just that gut instinct that told me something was off. I asked where I could sign and then went to wait in the truck. When he came out a while later, he was livid and started berating me, telling me what a rude bitch I was. I turned to face him and said, "Yeah, and you are having sex with *her*." The look on his face was etched in my memory for a long time. He was so caught off guard he didn't have time to make up a story. He just asked, "How did you know?" Well, that was answer enough for me. I told him he had one day to get his things, or perhaps I said, "Shit" and "Get out of the house." I found out shortly after that he had gotten this one pregnant. So, the marriage, which never should have happened in the first place, was now over, four months after the "I dos were said and the ink was dry." I felt like I was in an ocean with wave after wave crashing into me and not being able to come up for air.

The woman he got pregnant and later married had the nerve to pick my daughter up one day with a shirt on indicating how far along she was in her pregnancy. I believe she intended to let me know they had slept together while he was still married to me (I had already figured that one out). She also had the nerve to say if I had paid more attention to him, he might not have cheated on me. I believe she thought it was a competition and she had won. But I do remember through the tears and hurt thinking, "You win, you can have him!" Giving attention to a man who put me down as much as he did was not something he deserved.

This man put me through hell. His emotional and mental abuse towards me, his constant philandering, put-downs, lack of compassion and kindness, racism, rude comments, and the absence of love towards me did far more damage than I ever knew until recently. He told me I was fat (even though I was ninety-eight pounds), I was ugly, and the typical "No one will ever love you." He would gaslight me, would say it was all in my

Hurt, Lies, Disbelief

head, and would call me crazy when I questioned him on who he was sleeping with, or where he had been 'til all hours of the night. I try to live my life without regrets because they don't serve me; however, this is one of two regrets I have in my life. Marrying him was one of the worst choices I could have made. But that would have changed everything as I know it. And who's to say that would have been better?

This same man went to the bar every Wednesday night for ladies' night right up to and after I gave birth. So, on that Wednesday night in December while he was at the bar doing whatever it was that he did, I was at home, cleaning my bathtub. I was "nesting," which is an overwhelming desire to get your home ready for the new baby within a couple of weeks before you go into labour. Just after midnight that same night I went into labour and had my daughter the following day.

I had been a stay-at-home mom while married, but I put on my big girl panties and found a good job within three days of him moving out. I found a day home in my townhouse complex for my daughter. Then, shortly after, she and I moved down the block to an apartment complex where I became the

Cut The Anchor

maintenance manager. This allowed me subsidized rent. My ex then moved back into the original townhouse we had shared so we could co-parent for a period of time before he moved in with and married *her*. I was twenty-one years old. He told me many times during this period that he was going to steal my daughter and take her to Ontario where he was from. I had people in the complex on high alert, letting me know if anything looked out of the ordinary. I was petrified that I would come to pick her up one day and she would be gone. It's funny how some things stay with us over the years. This feels like it happened yesterday.

I don't know how I got through all of this. I just kept thinking, "Put one foot in front of the other. You have a daughter to raise." Stuffing everything down and never telling anyone how I was feeling and what I was going through seemed to be my thing. Was this because I didn't know how I felt, or was it because a part of me thought I deserved it, or was I just so broken that I was embarrassed to let anyone know the truth behind the outwardly happy, strong, smiling person they saw? Do you mask your sadness from your loved ones? Or perhaps you keep yourself so busy that you mask it from yourself.

Hurt, Lies, Disbelief

A while after the divorce, I started dating another man. At this point my daughter and I were living in that apartment complex I was managing. I walked in one day to find him having sex with another woman in my bed! Yet another event to stuff deep down and not deal with.

Again, I thought, "Why does this black cloud keep following me around?"

I was so insecure and desperate to be loved that I started making many poor choices, all to do with men. I never wanted to be alone, so I went from dating or marrying one man to another. I dated a man for a short time and became pregnant. I told him, and his response was "I haven't told you yet, but I have cancer. So, I won't be around to help you. Maybe you should have an abortion." Well, he didn't have cancer, and he didn't die, but an abortion is exactly what I had. That same friend that took me to have my stomach pumped now took me to have an abortion. It was very painful, and I was sick for at least a week. I didn't think about it much after. I know some women who have had an abortion, and it did have a negative impact on their lives after the fact. This did not happen for me, perhaps because I never allowed myself to think or reflect on what had happened. Or what had been done to me. I didn't take my decision lightly; I just felt it was the right thing to do for me and my life at the time.

Now, enter the two men in my life who did a number on me, off and on, for around fourteen years. I met one of them online. I still remember what he was wearing the day we met, where we met, and how the first date went. Which was amazing. I remember thinking, "Wow, this guy is great. I want to know more about him." Well, great he was. At lying, cheating, manipulating, using his charm to get what he wanted, and telling me what he knew I needed to hear. There is so much that this man did to me that I will only touch on the big things. To me, he was like a drug, and I couldn't get enough of him. I really to this day don't understand the hold that he had on me for so many years. Hopefully one day I will understand what it was about him. The research I did on drugs told me that most people will feel intense euphoria while high on stimulants. It's almost as if they can do anything and everything. Senses are heightened, and mood is at an all-time high. Yes! This was exactly how I felt when I was with him. Until I wasn't. Then it was like I crashed. I would get down, beat myself up for being with him, be angry at him, be angry

Hurt, Lies, Disbelief

at myself, just be angry in general. I couldn't even talk to anyone about him because we were in a secret relationship. How messed up is that?

When we first started dating, he told me he was divorced. I had been at his house, and he seemed to be telling me the truth, I didn't see any signs of a woman living there. Not long after, though, I got a call from his wife. Yes, that's correct, his wife. What the hell? Without going into detail, I told him, "Never call or text me again, don't come to my house, and don't email me. I want nothing to do with you." I never gave him the chance to explain. I was just so done with the lies. He tried, but I stood my ground and wouldn't listen to what he had to say.

Then a girlfriend of mine who knew him told me, "He is divorced. His ex is just a bit on the crazy side." Whether she was "crazy" or just sick of his lies, I am not sure. But, about a year or more later, I ran into him at a pub. When I came outside, he had slipped his number under the wiper blade of my car. I didn't call him right away, but, like I said, he was a drug. When I did call him, we started seeing each other again.

Cut The Anchor

I was cleaning houses for a living at the time, so I would clean his house every two weeks. While cleaning one day, I saw a rental agreement on his counter (right there in plain view). It was for a rental in Phoenix, and it had a woman's name on it beside his. When I confronted him, he said she was his golf buddy, and they were going to Phoenix to golf. Yeah, right! So, again I stopped seeing him for a while, only to be roped back in a year later. I was always a secret girlfriend of his. He said it was because our kids were similar ages and he didn't want them to know about us. At the time, I agreed because I didn't want my kids to know either. Now I realize I was a secret because he had a girlfriend. Then, while cleaning his house another time, I found a picture and card that a little person had made saying, "I love you like a dad." It was folded in half beside a picture of him and a woman who was definitely someone close to him. So, back to the shop (where he was working at the time) I went to confront him yet again. He had another excuse, and I don't remember what it was, but I left him again. This happened many times over the years. He just kept pulling me back in. I realize I had choices, but at the time I was broken, and he gave me what I needed. Or so I thought.

Hurt, Lies, Disbelief

Now the hard part of the truth begins. We were at our usual restaurant eating lunch when he informed me that he had gotten engaged to the same woman who was on the rental agreement years before. I don't remember that drive home. All I remember is crying so hard I couldn't see. I was heading to Canmore that day with my daughter and friends to train for our mountain race coming up. I sat in the back seat with my non-see-through mug and got very drunk. I am not a big drinker, but I was that day. And yes, that drug pulled me back in about six months later. We continued the affair until one day again at our usual place he informed me he had gotten married a couple of weeks prior. This time I was done for good. Or was I?

I didn't see or talk to him for a couple of years, and then he informed me he was getting divorced. Shocker. And, yet again, there he was on my doorstep, and I stupidly let him in *again*. About a month later we were out having dinner and his phone lit up. Due to the big font I could see the text said, "Hey babe, what are you up to?" It shouldn't have surprised me, but it did. I said, "Take me home, and don't ever call me again." This time I meant it. I blocked him from everything I could think of. I was finally strong enough to never go down that path again with him or anyone else. I guess I am a slow learner, but I was just so head over heels for him. And, like I said, I have no idea why. It took so long to get him out of my system.

I now knew what it felt like to be the "other woman," and it felt horrible! I am not making excuses for what I did; I made many mistakes, and I now own them all.

The second man was not married and was the one cheating on me and several other women. Many of us at the same time, which I found out later. This man, like the other one, is a narcissist, incapable of loving someone other than himself, and is a master manipulator, but he has all the other qualities that I am looking for in a man. We had so much in common, including things we liked to do, our childhood, families we grew up in, our spirituality, our kids were the same ages and were friends, his grandkids were the same ages as mine, we thought the same way on many topics, and so much more. He told me one time the reason he couldn't be with me was because I challenged him to be a better man. I push him to go deep inside, to learn and grow and transform. He said he just wanted to be with women who let him do whatever he wanted

Hurt, Lies, Disbelief

and never challenged him. He liked the simpler ones, he told me.

He told me many times he loved me, but his actions spoke louder than his words. We lived down the street from one another, and I would drive by his house at 5:45 a.m. while heading to yoga. On one occasion there was a white SUV in his driveway. I asked him about it, and his response was it was the Telus guy. I said, "Funny a Telus guy is at your house at 5:45 am." Busted! I ended up referring to this woman as "the SUV girl"; there were so many I had to label them. This time, however, I didn't stay with him. That was the end of us! And the SUV remained in his driveway.

There was another woman, previous to the SUV girl, he was with for a year unknown to me. I received many horrible phone calls from her letting me know he had been sharing her bed for the last year. She was screaming at me, wanting to know everything about him and me, stating she deserved to be told. I didn't engage with her. Instead, I told her if she continued to harass me, I would call the police. That ended the phone calls from her. In total, that I know of, there were four women that he was with throughout our secret relationship. Yes, this

Cut The Anchor

one was a secret too. And the reasons were similar to the other man's: because our kids were friends, he didn't want them to know about us. I, on the other hand, told my kids about this one. They all liked him and would have welcomed him into our family with open arms. I do understand now why both of these men wanted secret relationships—so they could have many relationships all at the same time. I probably knew it deep down but didn't want to admit it to myself.

Both of these men did so much damage to my mental and emotional well-being for so long. And yes, I realize the secret part was due to the fact they were both with other women, whether married or just dating. I just didn't know it at the time. I haven't fully come to terms with the hold they each had on me. But I believe my low self-esteem and self-loathing played a huge part. I found the men I gravitated to most were the ones that took a lot of work to get them to pay attention to me. The ones that liked me right away felt boring or foreign. I didn't know what to do with that type of partner. I needed the one that made me work for it, made me feel like shit, and made me feel like they were doing me a favor by being with me. Because to that point that was all I knew. Does any of this resonate with

Hurt, Lies, Disbelief

you? Have you been in a situation where you were with someone who was clearly very toxic for you, but you stayed anyway? What were your reasons? Were they similar to mine or completely different?

What I did learn through all this is that these men were broken and in turn projected their feelings of inadequacies onto me. I was enough. Actually, more than enough. I just didn't figure that out until this year. At this point in my life, there is no place in my heart for blame or hatred. Whether it is towards myself for the part I played with infidelities or towards these men who did it to me. But I was full of blame and had hatred towards myself and them for years. I hated myself. Because how could I do to another woman what had been done to me so many times? I was so incredibly hurt every time I got cheated on. How could I have done this to another woman? Not making excuses, but perhaps I became the "hurter" to avoid being the "hurt." I believe I compartmentalized the relationship. I didn't think about her when I was with him. But I did think about her when I wasn't. I have worked through this in therapy, readings, journalling, and self-discovery courses. I can't change what I did; all I can do is learn from my mistakes and grow to be a better person, which is the path I am currently on. I did, however, save the insurmountable blame for my biggest infidelity, which cost me far more than I ever knew or thought possible.

> *They didn't cheat because of who you are.*
> *They chose to cheat because of who they are not.*
> *Charles J. Orlando*

UNRAVELING TOXIC RELATIONSHIPS

Have you ever felt left out of friendships? Or are you the one that leaves people out of your friend groups? Do you keep picking the wrong partner? Do you wonder when the right person or tribe is going to come along? I have felt left out for as long as I can remember. Starting with my family unit, girlfriends from school, groups of women as an adult, and even with my kids at times. Have you been in a similar situation yourself? How did it make you feel?

Cut The Anchor

My beliefs about myself in my twenties and part of my thirties were that I was unlovable and never good enough, which spilled into my relationships with men, my family, and my female friends. This constant feeling of never being good enough was compounded every time I was so easily cast aside by men and women. What was it about me that people disliked? Why was it so easy to cast me aside as if I didn't exist? I heard so many times that people didn't know quite how to take me. I had been told I was blunt, abrupt, and rude at times. However, I saw myself as a to-the-point, truthful, and a no-bullshit kind of person.

This, I have learned over the years, can rub some the wrong way. I, for one, would prefer to be around someone who is blunt and to the point so you always know where you stand with them rather than the fakeness I feel many people live by. The rumors floated around that I was hard to get along with. I didn't understand this because I felt I was very open, kind, and caring. However, looking back, I was guarded, angry, and had a chip on my shoulder. I was always looking for a fight, ready with retaliation when hurtful words were thrown, and I had expectations of others to be perfect, which went both ways. The need for myself to be perfect

Unraveling Toxic Relationships

was all-consuming. I realize now that I was in survival mode for most of my life. So many things had happened to me that I was constantly on the defensive. It was how I protected myself.

I felt I had been put down so much that I was constantly working hard to prove my worth. It was as if I was begging to be liked and accepted just as I was. And I realize now that can be exhausting to be around. It is also an exhausting way to live!

I remember being at the lake with a boyfriend and his family when he asked me why I was cutting the carrots that way. I slammed the knife down and said, "Cut the carrots any fucking way you want," and I stormed off. His mom and sister were in shock. They didn't know what had just transpired. Nor did he. And sitting here now I don't either. Tears are running down my face as I laugh while writing this because some might call me crazy, and I would have to agree it was on the crazy side. However, in my mind at the time it was yet another put-down that I just couldn't take. I blew! I now know he was just asking a simple question about cutting carrots. How the mind can take things in, swirl them around, and turn them into something that was never meant to be hurtful is powerful. I

Cut The Anchor

pushed people away if they tried to get too close. I loved from afar. It was easier than being constantly hurt. The hurt turned into resentment, which turned into anger, which led to detachment and then into loneliness for the better part of my life.

My first love was when I was in grade ten and he was in grade twelve. He had been my sister's friend and knew my family quite well. I really wasn't into dating when I was younger, but while at a bush party, he revealed that he liked me. I remember this like it was yesterday. Before my sister and I headed out to the party, and I do believe it was the first time I had gone to a bush party, my mom and sister wanted to put makeup on me. I wasn't that girl; I was more into muscle magazines and car racing. But I let them put it on me; it made them feel better, and I didn't care either way. Once at the party, I remember him and me talking, and then he started to walk up a small hill before turning around and saying, "Don't you get it, I like you." No one up to that point had ever liked me or told me that they did. So, I was a bit shocked, especially because he was two years older.

We did start dating, and I remember feeling special because he would pick me up in his red Mustang

Unraveling Toxic Relationships

and drive me to school. All the girls were envious. He was great to me, and I did feel cared about. We dated for a year, but because his ex-girlfriend and her friend were so horrible to me, I ended up breaking it off. I would come home to spray paint on my sidewalk in front of my parents' home saying I was a slut and all sorts of other cruel things. He worked at Bowness Park, running the rides. He would get to work, and the girls had spray-painted awful things about me on the fence where the rides were. They also started doing damage to his red Mustang. One time at school, word went around that there was going to be a fight after school, and, apparently, it was with me and the ex-girlfriend's best friend. Well, I hate violence of any kind, so at the end of the day, I just walked out the side door and got on the bus. The joke was on them. I loved him, but I thought it would be easier if we parted ways so that we both didn't have to endure the torment they were putting us through.

More hurt continued to happen in my life. This one was definitely a big one. I was eighteen and living with a girlfriend at the time. We were both into rodeos and decided to go to the Red Deer rodeo an hour and a half south of where we lived. Her boyfriend at the time and his friend wanted to come as well but didn't have a place to stay and said all the hotel rooms were booked. They asked to stay in our hotel room. I said yes, as long as no one slept in my bed except me. I was adamant about this! After a night of drinking, dancing, and partying, we all went back to the hotel room, partied for a bit more, and then went to sleep. The friend slept in a chair, and my roommate's boyfriend slept with her, leaving my bed just for me. Or so I thought. I woke up to my roommate's boyfriend raping me. He had one hand over my mouth and the other hand around my wrists. He wasn't a big guy, but I couldn't push him off. I was in complete and utter shock! I felt paralyzed. He kept saying, "You want it." Then he said, "You can't say anything. No one will believe you." And he was right, no one did!!

I just kept thinking, "What did I do that made him think I wanted this? Did I do something, did I say something? Why would he be doing this to me?" I was in utter shock and disbelief. On the drive home the next day, I told my roommate what happened, and her boyfriend was right: she didn't believe me. She said I had cheated with him, and now I was turning it around saying he raped me. I was stunned. I couldn't believe what I was hearing.

Unraveling Toxic Relationships

I moved out within a week and moved in with my boyfriend who became my first husband. Yes, the philanderer one. I did not tell him what happened. I am not sure why. Perhaps I was afraid he wouldn't believe me either, or maybe in some mixed-up way, I felt it was my fault somehow.

Then years later, when I married my second husband, he also knew the guy, so I told him what had happened, and he also didn't believe me. He said, "He wouldn't have done that. He's a nice guy." This guy was well-known in the community. Again, I was in disbelief that two people didn't believe me. I never told another soul until fifteen years later.

While having coffee with a guy I trained with, who happened to be a policeman at the time, I opened up and told him what had happened. He said I should make a statement even though it was past the Limitations Act. He said this way if he ever did it again, they would have it on file. I never went in to make that statement. I am not sure why, but perhaps I thought because two people I cared about didn't believe me, why would anyone else?

Sexual assaults are a topic all on their own, and the stats are staggering. All I can say is, from personal

Cut The Anchor

experience, it never really leaves you. I remember bowling one night with a friend and his kids. We were having a great time, and in walked HIM. He was with his kids and ended up in the lane right beside us. Apparently, I turned green and told my friend I had to go. I ended up playing piano that night well into the early hours of the next day. This was my therapy, and I was very grateful I had that outlet.

Another time, I had gone country dancing with the "carrot guy"—yes, we were still friends after the carrot incident. We were having fun, and all of a sudden, HE walked in, and I started to shake and said we needed to leave.

The final one though happened not long ago. I was in Costco buying myself flowers when I walked around the corner and ran right into him. He appeared to not even know who I was. I, on the other hand, couldn't get out fast enough. I was shaking and by the time I got home was sick to my stomach. I thought I had put all that behind me, but apparently, I hadn't. I cried for a few days and couldn't quite get it together.

Being violated in this way is something you really can't explain. You have to experience it, and that

Unraveling Toxic Relationships

is an experience I wouldn't wish on anyone. Have you been sexually assaulted in any way? Did it leave you feeling empty? Did you feel it was your fault? Did you wonder what you had done for them to do this to you? Did you know the person, or was it someone random? These are all questions to take an in-depth look at and acknowledge how you truly felt. Talking about it and not letting it rot inside has helped me, and perhaps it would help you too. It has nagged at me over the years, and I wondered why I never reported him, but looking at these stats it makes a little more sense why I didn't.

According to a study done by the Justice Institute of British Columbia, all people are potential victims, regardless of gender, age, race, religion, sexual orientation, or education. One in every seventeen Canadian women is raped at some point in her life. A woman is sexually assaulted by forced intercourse every seventeen minutes in Canada. This is staggering to me! Girls and young women between the ages of fifteen and twenty-four are the most likely victims. Eighty percent of assaults happen in the victim's home, and seventy percent of rapes are committed by a perpetrator who knows the victim (relative, friend, neighbor, colleague, or other acquaintance).

Cut The Anchor

Statistics Canada has found that one in four girls and one in eight boys have been sexually abused by the time they are eighteen. These stats are only the ones reported and are considered to be much higher.

According to Statistics Canada, only one in five sexual assault cases substantiated by Canadian police end up in court. About one in ten substantiated sexual assault cases result in a conviction.

Understanding the reasons behind this underreporting is complex and multifaceted.

Victims of sexual assault often encounter various barriers that deter them from reporting, including the following:

1. Stigma and shame: Society's tendency to blame or shame victims can make survivors reluctant to come forward due to fear of judgment.
2. Fear of retaliation: Victims might fear retaliation or harm from the perpetrator, especially if they know each other.
3. Trauma and psychological impact: The trauma of sexual assault can lead to psychological distress, which might hinder

a survivor's ability to navigate the reporting process.
4. Distrust of authorities: Some victims fear they won't be taken seriously or that their cases won't be handled appropriately by law enforcement.
5. Lack of support: Many victims lack support systems that could encourage them to report the assault.
6. Complex legal process: Legal proceedings can be daunting, with potential traumatization during the process.
7. Perceived futility: The low conviction rate can lead victims to believe that reporting won't yield justice.
8. Cultural and societal factors: Cultural norms and societal expectations can impact a victim's decision to report.

Addressing this issue requires a multifaceted approach that includes destigmatizing the reporting process, enhancing victim support services, improving law enforcement training, and increasing awareness about consent and sexual assault. By fostering an environment that supports and believes in survivors, we can hope to close the gap between reported and unreported cases, offering a greater

Cut The Anchor

chance for justice and recovery. I believe I didn't report it for a few of the reasons listed, #1, 3, and 5 for sure.

A few years later, I met and married my second husband, who I loved but not enough. I knew he would be a good dad, and he is. I thought he was funny. He was hard-working and would always stop to help someone in need. These were traits I was looking for. I wanted more kids, and I didn't want them to be too far apart in age, and the biggest reason was I just knew in my heart he would never cheat on me, and he didn't. But sadly, that isn't a good enough reason to get married, and I now own that. Our marriage wasn't horrible, and it gave us two great sons, but it wasn't what it could have been. I was fifth in the pecking line. It went work, cattle, his immediate family, our boys, then my daughter and me. I didn't want to be fifth, I wanted to be first, and not only did I want this, I deserved it. After five years of marriage and a total of seven years together, I left.

Things went from bad to worse at this point. He stopped paying child support, so I had to get a lawyer. He stopped hauling water to our home, where I was now living, as he moved to the

Unraveling Toxic Relationships

farmhouse. He stopped plowing the snow to the house, and he cut me off his gas card (without telling me). Basically, the kids and I were on our own. I was without a job, no money, no family, and too proud to ask for help. I think the thing I hated him for most was that during mediation he informed me he would no longer be taking my daughter when he took the boys because "she looks like you and I despise you." This hurt on so many levels as he was the one my daughter called Daddy. She was two when we met, and she loved him. He treated her like a daughter, and then, all of a sudden, he wanted nothing to do with her. It broke my heart, and I felt like it was all my fault because I just kept picking men who weren't good.

The first Christmas after he said he wouldn't take her, he brought garbage bags full of gifts to her when he dropped the boys off. She was nine years old, but she looked at the gifts and said, "I don't want your gifts. Take them with you."

After the second marriage ended, I got into a three-year relationship. He always wanted me to dress a certain way, which I found out later was because the ex he was still in love with dressed that way. He was basically a cranky person, he was extremely

Cut The Anchor

cheap (frugal, good, cheap, bad), he never paid for anything when it came to my kids, and he even had my daughter pay for ice cream for her and her brothers one night while I was teaching piano. She was ten at the time! The final straw was when he asked if he could go back and try with his ex, and I replied, "Absolutely, you can go back and try." When it didn't work with her, as I knew it wouldn't, he came back and said, "Okay, I now know I want to be with you."

I said, "Oh no, that ship has sailed." He said I tricked him. "Nope, I said you could go try. I never said you could come back if it didn't work." And that was the end of him.

Then the real abusive one happened. He was fifteen years older, and the reason I started dating him was because he wasn't cheap like my last relationship. He wined and dined me and bought me and my kids things (money had never been a reason for me to date, but it was nice to feel special). I remember the first time he came over and brought pizza for me and my kids. I asked him what I owed him, and he said, "What do you mean? It's nothing. It's just pizza." I just wasn't used to it because of my previous boyfriend. He took me shopping and bought me

Unraveling Toxic Relationships

nice things, he took me to fancy restaurants I had never been to, and he introduced me to things I had never been exposed to, like opera, jazz, fine foods, fine wine, and more.

I realized later that he had pulled me into his web by essentially buying my affection. The nice guy act didn't last long, though, as the abuse started soon after. At first, it was mental and emotional, and in the end, it turned physical. He made me buy a new house (the one I was in that I had purchased with my own money from my divorce was apparently too small—it was perfect for me and my kids though). And remember I was still a lost soul, with no confidence or self-worth, and I was still anorexic and depressed. So, I purchased the bigger home on the golf course with the hard-earned money from my first home. He then proceeded to try to take it away from me and the kids. He was a realtor and a mortgage broker, and the house was bought for sale by owner. I wasn't part of the deal, even though it was all my money. None of it was his. When I went to sign the papers, everything was in his name. *Nothing* was in mine. He somehow managed to get his name only on the title and his name only on the mortgage.

Cut The Anchor

This is when the abuse heightened. He would threaten all the time that he would kick me and the kids out and change the locks if I didn't do what I was told. He would say, "Little girl, little girl, you know I can kick you out at any point, and you and the kids will have nowhere to go." He was extremely controlling, and through these two years of hell, I was mentally and verbally abused on a daily basis. I was told when to go to bed, when to eat, what to eat, and what to wear. I had to sit in a certain chair every night for my nightly lecture on what a horrible, useless bitch I was. I wasn't allowed to do certain things like paint any walls in MY house or use sharp knives (maybe he thought I might stab him in his sleep). I had to keep my eight-year-old twin boys quiet at all times. He worked from home, so that was quite difficult, and if they weren't quiet, I was lectured that night. I wasn't allowed any friends over, nor could I talk to them on the phone, and I was way too proud to tell anyone what was going on.

But with abusers, they start off slowly. They start to pull you away from your friends and family. They want you all to themselves, so when the abuse starts you have no one but them. An abuser does not start out by hitting you one day. No, they start out by

Unraveling Toxic Relationships

manipulating you, gaslighting you, and making you feel like it is all your fault and all in your head. After four months, he moved his depressed brother in. His brother didn't work, and at this point, I was paying all the bills. I didn't get monetary help from either one of them.

I was only allowed to leave the house if I was going to work at the school, work out at the gym, or run errands, but he always had to know exactly where I was at all times. I felt like a prisoner in my own home. No one knew what was going on because I was too embarrassed to tell anyone. I couldn't believe I had gotten myself into this position. He even forced me to change my will so he would get everything. Once the will was done, however, I went behind his back and had the will changed back to the original one. I explicitly told the lawyer's office not to call the house when the will was ready. I told them to call my cell, but they didn't do that, and when I was working at my boy's school as a noon-hour supervisor, I saw him walking towards me, enraged. I had a very good idea of what had happened, and I had to lie and calm him down, saying the lawyer was just changing the guardianship of my kids. I was constantly on guard and worried all the time about doing or saying the wrong thing. I was living a nightmare and no one knew. Or so I thought.

Recently, I was talking with one of my sons and the topic came up. My son informed me that he knew all along and that he had heard the yelling and the abuse. I always thought I had kept my kids in the dark, but I guess they knew. I was sick when I discovered this. I felt I let them down as a mother—not protecting them from hearing the verbal abuse that I endured.

As I mentioned, one of the places I was allowed to go was the gym. This worked in my favour. I started going for three hours a day, I worked out with the cop I talked about, and he got me into bodybuilding. I also ended up being a fitness coach, all because I was being abused, and the only solace I had was at the gym. I have always tried to find the good in every situation, and this was the good from this one. Fitness changed my life!

This man was a con artist, and I didn't figure this out until it was too late. He took the woman before me for a quarter of a million dollars. She came to my door one day to try and warn me, but he had manipulated me so badly that I didn't believe her

Unraveling Toxic Relationships

until he did it to me. I was able to get everything back in my name because of a guardian angel at the bank. She knew what he was like because she had dealt with him before. While at her office one day, she asked if I was okay. I said, "Of course I am. What do you mean?"

She closed her office door and said, "I am concerned and really want to know if you are okay." Because I believed her, I broke down and told her what he had done with the house and the title of the home. I honestly don't know how she did it, but with the help of a lawyer and my paper trail of the money, she was able to get everything back in my name with his name on nothing. This took time, though, and I had to put up with the abuse for another year.

I remember the day I got the papers from the bank; it was the Friday of the July long weekend. We were on the phone, and he was yelling at me for something while I was driving home from the gym. I hung up and called a friend (I only had two at this point, and they were boyfriend/girlfriend). I called them to see if they were going to the lake and, if so, could I come? I said I couldn't go home, and I didn't have anything with me. They said, "Just come over, and we will take care of it." So, off I went. All three of my kids were at their dads' for the weekend. I had an amazing weekend for the first time in two years. When I got home on the Sunday night (he hadn't known where I was all weekend, so he was livid), he started the whole "little girl" thing, and I flipped open the papers and said, "This is actually my house, and you can get the F out." Not well played on my part, as I should have had someone there with me. He chased me into the bedroom. I had slammed the door shut and locked it, but he kicked it down, and that was when it got physical. He did end up leaving three days later, but he made me pay seventeen thousand for the apparent work he put into the house. At that point I didn't have any fight left in me, so I paid him. I was completely broken and a shell of a person by then.

You would think I would have given up by this point. But I desperately wanted to feel loved. I didn't date anyone for two years, but next up was the one that broke my heart. I truly loved him, and he hurt me. He lived in Fort St John, so it was a long-distance relationship. The deal was that he would stay living up there until his daughter graduated, which would be the following year. We met in January, got serious in May, and it was the following June when he would move to Sherwood

Unraveling Toxic Relationships

Park, and we would build a house together. That did not happen, and my heart was broken again.

Then came those two off-and-on-again relationships, which I call cocaine. Yes, I made the choice to be with them, but they knew how broken I was, and they used that to their advantage, and I was addicted. What did they have? They had power, manipulation, narcissistic traits, and this crazy hold on me that I don't know if I will ever fully understand. They said what I needed to hear and did what I needed them to do. They knew I was vulnerable and broken, and they took advantage of that. I finally found the strength to end it with both of them in 2018. Of course, they still tried many times to gaslight me and get me back in their web. They called, texted, and left flowers at my door. I would block them on social media, emails, and my phone, but they still found ways to get through to me. I never responded to them and never gave them a reason to think they could come back, but the narcissism in them allowed them to continue to try. I stood my ground, and I am now completely free of them. They do not have a hold on me. I feel like I am five years sober from my relationship addiction to them both.

Cut The Anchor

Have you ever felt addicted to someone that treated you badly? It could be a significant other, a friend, a parent, or anyone who treats you badly, but you just keep going back for more. If this is you, it might be time to take a really good look at your limiting self-beliefs. I know that's what helped me.

I definitely tended to have a bad taste in men. If there were ninety-nine great men in a room and one bad, I would continually seek out that one bad one. This was basically my whole life to this point. I was constantly trying to find love from a man because I didn't feel I had it growing up. I also didn't love myself, and I now know love has to come from within before you can ever seek it from someone else. I knew I needed to work on myself before I could ever be with someone long-term. So, the tough work began and is still ongoing.

Regrettably, the hurtfulness extended not only to relationships with men but also to my interactions with women. Being consistently excluded from groups, whether large or small, has been a recurring theme throughout my life, from my early years to the present. I've overheard supposed "friends" talking about me behind my back, experienced betrayal and hurtful actions from women, and

Unraveling Toxic Relationships

found myself left out of gatherings—even when I was part of the initial text chat planning. There were instances when I was initially included in get-togethers, only to be gradually phased out without any explanation.

The reasons behind this exclusion remain a mystery. Was it rooted in jealousy or something else entirely? I've pondered this question countless times. Have you ever found yourself in a similar situation with your circle of friends? Have you experienced the bewildering sensation of being left out without understanding why? It's disheartening to witness how women can sometimes treat each other unkindly, especially when the potential to uplift and empower one another is far greater.

Do you experience feelings of exclusion, and if so, how have you navigated through those situations? It's crucial that we work together to build each other up rather than allowing division to break us apart.

I've reached a point where I no longer allow such individuals to affect me negatively. Recognizing my own value, I've deliberately chosen to be in the company of people who are kind, inclusive, and understanding—individuals who possess empathy and compassion. This shift in perspective and circle of friends has been empowering. Maybe this transformation is partly rooted in my personal experiences. Having been on the receiving end of exclusion, I've developed a strong inclination to ensure others are never left out. I've known firsthand the pain of feeling isolated, and I'm committed to preventing others from experiencing that same hurt.

Would you agree that surrounding oneself with empathetic and inclusive individuals is not only a reflection of self-worth but also a way to create a positive and nurturing environment for everyone?

I always take good from a bad situation; otherwise, the situation is a waste of time, and I don't like to waste my time in life. So, the good I took away from those abusive relationships is that it was the start of my new life journey. It pushed me to start working on myself and figure out why I allowed men to control me and what my part was in choosing these men. And so, the Kari Journey began.

Unraveling Toxic Relationships

*A good relationship is when someone
accepts your past
supports your present
and encourages your future.*

Zig Ziglar

*If he makes you lose your family,
lose your friends, lose your confidence,
lose your self-esteem, or lose your
happiness
then you NEED to lose him.*

Author unknown

GOING IT ALONE

Are you a single parent? Have you been one in the past? Do you know single parents? Or perhaps you grew up in a single-parent home?

After the breakup of my brief marriage to my first husband, I found myself a single mother to my fourteen-month-old daughter. At the age of twenty-one, we parted ways, a decision driven by the need to escape a toxic marriage riddled with loneliness, infidelity, mental and emotional abuse, and prolonged periods of silent treatment. Determined to provide for my

Cut The Anchor

daughter's well-being, I swiftly found employment at a medical lab, working from 3-9 p.m. This arrangement allowed for a limited time at the day home each day, easing the demands of parenthood. Initially, my daughter and I settled into an apartment a few blocks away, allowing me to benefit from subsidized rent while looking after the other units in the building. After a span of three months, I moved back to our townhome, as my ex moved in with the woman who was pregnant with his child. I still took care of the apartment building, but living in the townhouse made more sense as her day home was in that complex. I adjusted my work schedule to 7-3 p.m. so that she could stay at the same day home. My mornings began at 5:30 a.m., getting her ready, dropping her off, and making my way to work downtown. The evening routine was a repetition of picking her up, playing with her, and getting ready for the following day. This cycle took its toll, compounded by my battle with depression and anorexia.

With no family residing nearby, as they all lived in Calgary, the responsibility rested solely on my shoulders. Being an inherently protective mom, I hesitated to get babysitters, trusting only my

Going It Alone

parents, the daycare provider, and occasionally her dad—though even that was met with apprehension due to the fear he might take her to Ontario as previously mentioned. Consequently, my social life was severely curtailed during this phase of my life. However, amid the challenges, I was fortunate to have a very supportive friend. He remained by my side following the divorce, a contrast to others who seemed compelled to take sides. It's intriguing how people often find themselves picking sides in such situations. I've observed instances where individuals maintained relationships solely to avoid losing mutual friends. In my case, this friend was a much-needed support. His care extended to my daughter as well. He was the same friend who took me to the hospital to have my stomach pumped after my suicide attempt.

At the age of twenty-eight, I found myself entering single parenthood once again, this time responsible for not just my daughter but also my twin boys, aged three, while my daughter was now eight and a half. Admittedly, it was an arduous journey, yet I had made this choice, and that left no room to dwell on the challenges. I had a mission to fulfill, and I embraced it wholeheartedly. At that point, my livelihood relied on a dried floral business, teaching piano to a handful of students, and occasionally babysitting. Regrettably, despite my efforts, these pursuits proved insufficient to sustain us.

After enduring about six months of cohabitation following our separation, my husband eventually moved into the farmhouse, leaving me with the kids in our home. A series of actions followed that left me struggling. He stopped hauling water to our house, which meant I had to resort to transporting buckets of water from a friend's place located forty-five minutes away just to provide basic necessities for the kids. He also refused to plow the road from the secondary highway onto our property, making it increasingly difficult for us to leave our home. This situation, coupled with the halt of the gas card he provided, left me in a dire predicament. I had to plead with the workers who plowed the oil wells on our property, offering them homemade cookies and banana bread as incentives to keep our access road plowed when it snowed. The gas card dilemma was equally distressing, catching me off guard when it failed to work at the gas station. I vividly remember sitting in the van, overwhelmed with emotion as I struggled with the uncertainty of how I would afford the gas. Child support payments began sporadically, only to be halted once more

Going It Alone

shortly after they started. Faced with the urgency of securing financial stability for my kids, I made the difficult decision to seek legal help. Engaging a lawyer was a daunting task given my limited financial resources, but I knew it was essential. Swallowing my pride, I asked my dad for the $2,000 retainer fee, a sum that felt monumental to me at the time. Realizing that the farm was no longer a viable option, I moved with my kids to Fort Saskatchewan and rented a home from a friend. The transition was swift—within hours of moving in on December 13th, I managed to unpack everything and set up the Christmas decorations and tree, and this marked the beginning of our new life. Remember, I was an overachiever and a perfectionist. Every picture was hung, every box was unpacked, and we were ready for Santa to come twelve days later.

After a year of separation, the day arrived for us to finalize the divorce. At 1 p.m. on a Wednesday, we both met with our respective lawyers to go over the necessary paperwork. The matter of child support had been established based on his current job wage. However, as we walked out of that meeting, he unexpectedly uttered words that sent a chill down my spine: "You should watch your back. I'm going to be able to watch every move you make."

Cut The Anchor

The statement left me puzzled and concerned. I wondered if he was planning on moving closer to the house I was renting. But it turned out to be something entirely different—he had taken a job right beside the frozen food business where I worked. Moreover, this job paid him five times more than his previous job. I was blindsided by this news. I quickly contacted my lawyer, who took immediate action to fix the situation. Eventually, he ended up paying the correct amount of child support based on his new salary. In the aftermath, I made a conscious choice not to engage in ongoing legal battles. I refrained from pursuing alimony, his pension, or claiming any portion of the farm. I could have gone back each year since he was a contract worker, but I chose not to do that. I wanted to show him that my intentions weren't rooted in financial gain, despite his dad's initial insinuation during the early days of our relationship. My strong desire for validation as a decent person persisted. Sadly, despite my intentions, he continued to perceive me as the one who had shattered our family unit. Yet, the reality was that I had pleaded with him for an entire year to seek counseling, a plea he consistently ignored. The consequences of his new job, with its demanding on-call schedule, meant that my twin boys could only spend five

Going It Alone

days a month at his house. This presented its own set of challenges. While I heard from other single parents who had family support and the luxury of alternating weeks off while caring for just one child, my circumstances were markedly different. With three children and no external assistance, those five days felt like a rare and cherished break. However, even those moments of reprieve were tainted by the fact that my daughter's interactions with her dad were becoming increasingly scarce due to his current wife's mistreatment of her.

After about three months we found a place to rent in Sherwood Park, but it was horrendous, so I did my best to make it our cozy little home until I could find something to purchase. Then in May of that same year, I found the perfect home for us to buy. It was a half-block walk to the school. I LOVED that home, and we moved in just before the August long weekend. We all had our own rooms, and I was able to do some renovations. It had a big backyard for the kids, we backed onto a park, and most of all, it was all mine. My first home. I was so proud. I did a lot of work painting and had new hardwood floors put in, new carpets, and new windows all in time. Now, you might be wondering where I found the funds for these renovations. By that point, the mobile home we had lived in on the farm had been sold, providing me with some money. I was also able to purchase our new home by assuming the existing mortgage.

During the time I was renting the home in Fort Saskatchewan, I took on the job at the frozen food business (the one my second husband worked near). Since the pay was less than satisfactory—barely enough to cover daycare expenses for my boys, after-school care for my daughter, food, and the cost of commuting—I encountered the question of why I would choose a job that didn't offer enough to make ends meet. Some might have suggested going on welfare or applying for food stamps, which are perfectly valid options for those in need. However, that wasn't the path I wanted to take. My pride wouldn't allow it. My perspective was rooted in the belief that sitting at home on welfare wasn't as appealing as being out in the world, actively working, networking, and exploring new opportunities. While I awaited the mythical "knock on the door" from destiny, I realized that waiting wouldn't lead to success. The reality was that no one was going to offer me a job out of the blue. So, I chose to take matters into my own hands. I saw this job not only as a way to support my family but

Going It Alone

also as a chance to connect with people, acquire new skills, and explore the world beyond my comfort zone. As it turned out, I eventually purchased that very business. And just like that, I stepped into the role of an entrepreneur, embracing a new chapter in my life's journey.

Despite living three hours away, my parents played a significant role in supporting my kids and me. Every summer, they took my kids for a few weeks, providing them with many great memories. They went the extra mile by buying back-to-school clothes and supplies, knowing that finances were tight on my end. My mom's sewing skills came in handy as she made dance clothes for a couple of my kids, and my dad ensured my hockey-playing son had the sticks he needed. On top of that, every visit they brought a care package filled with practical items like paper towels, toilet paper, Kraft dinner, peanut butter, and other treats. Their thoughtful gestures meant a lot, even though I might not have expressed my gratitude as much as I should have. They never made me feel ashamed of not being able to afford certain things.

I had always wanted to go to university while I was married the second time, but my second husband was against me going. And because he was the one making most of the money, and pretty much everything had to be his way, I never went. As soon as we separated, though, the first thing I did was enroll in interior design at the U of A. I got a subsidy and was able to attend. Despite the challenges of raising three kids, managing a frozen food business, teaching piano, catering, completing nightly homework, and trying to reclaim a sense of identity in my thirties, I embarked on a three-year journey of education. Looking back, I still wonder how I managed to juggle it all. My thirties brought their own struggles, and I began experiencing severe panic attacks. It was a frightening experience, especially when I had no idea what was happening. My dad had mentioned panic attacks before, which helped me recognize what I was going through. Eventually, I sought help and started taking anxiety medication, although asking for help was a huge step for me.

I worked around the kids' schedules for the most part, teaching piano during after-school hours and around their extracurricular activities. I worked my frozen food business during the day while they were at school and daycare, as well as the catering. I never missed a dance rehearsal, recital, or hockey

Going It Alone

game, I got my kids to bowling, art class, violin, sparks, Brownies, and gymnastics. I coached the boys' soccer, baked cookies, volunteered at the school for field trips, and allowed my kids to have sleepovers when they got older. The boys always had their own birthday parties; they didn't have to share one. When my daughter was twelve, she attended the Winnipeg School of Ballet. I lived in a very affluent community, where kids drove Mercedes to school. I was not, nor ever will be, a keep-up-with-the-Joneses kind of person, but I won't lie, it was very difficult raising my kids in such a wealthy community. My kids never asked me for things they knew I couldn't afford, but it broke my heart not to be able to give them basic things their friends had. My kids all acquired jobs at the age of fourteen so they could have the extra things they wanted. They have all told me as adults they are glad I couldn't hand things to them like their friends' parents did. They said they had to work hard for the items they purchased and appreciated their belongings, and they all have an incredible work ethic.

I always wanted our home to be the one all their friends wanted to come to. But that does come with a cost. Extra food and drinks were just not in my budget, and I felt incredibly bad. My kids knew

Cut The Anchor

they could have friends over; they just couldn't feed them. My kids never tried to make me feel bad, but I did, nonetheless. I remember my daughter's friend saying one time, "Oh cool, you have air conditioning."

My daughter laughed and said, "No, it is just thawing out from the winter. My mom keeps the place cold."

Truth be told, it was because I couldn't afford to heat my big house. I remember when they were young, I went without most things. I never got my hair done, never did my nails, didn't buy clothes, make-up, or shoes, and I didn't drink, smoke, or do much for myself. Those quarters, dimes, and nickels on the ground that people walk over? I picked those up, and that was how I bought extra things like cookies or other treats. Thank goodness I had learned the art of being frugal and great with money from my dad. I took in bottles, sold clothes the kids grew out of, and did whatever it took so my kids did not go without. I took them to movies and various outings, but we would either go to the dollar store for treats or I would make the treats and bring them in my purse. We went to the park a lot and had lots of picnics. There always seemed

Going It Alone

to be something that came up when raising my kids though. Clothes to purchase as they grew, endless shoes to buy, dance shoes and costumes, hockey equipment, field trip fees, birthday gifts for their friends' parties, and birthday parties to host, just to name a few. It just seemed endless, and when you don't have much coming in and no one else to count on it was extremely stressful. But I just kept putting one foot in front of the other and doing the best I could each day. Some days were better than others, but all I could do was try. Have you ever felt that way while raising your kids? Have you ever wished you could give them more than you did?

Christmas was always a very stressful time for me. I only had $150 to spend on each child, and that included the stockings. I had to be very creative. My kids were always very grateful for anything they got, but when the boys came home from their dad's, I knew he had spent anywhere between $1000-$2000 on them. It broke my heart because I couldn't do that for my daughter. It was the same for Easter and birthdays. I had to budget to afford the gifts.

I also made sure I did things with my kids separately so they felt important. It was during the lunch hour, and they got to choose what we did—bowling, restaurant, park—we would do whatever they picked. I would take turns with them, so they each got a day once a week. I also managed to save up money and take them all to Disneyland when they were thirteen, eight, and eight years old. It was tough, but I just really wanted to give them a good life and not have them suffer because I chose to get divorced. I saved up by taking in bottles, collected all the change I had in my purse at the end of each day, sold things around the house, and took on a couple more piano students, all so that we could have a holiday together.

If my kids wanted something big, they would have to research it, how much it was, how they could take care of it, etc., and really think about what they wanted it for. For example, when they wanted our dog, Ruxton, they came to me with a report written about what kind of dog, how much he was, their schedule for taking care of him, etc. We got the dog, and they completely helped with his care. It was not left for me to do—until they all moved out, that is. I wanted them to see you can't just buy something because you want it. You had to think about it and be sure it was something you really wanted.

Going It Alone

I tried to always be there for my kids when they needed me, and I would always go to bat for them when I knew they were in the right. I advocated for them when they needed me to, and I was a mama bear when someone hurt them or caused pain in any way. I know I sometimes embarrassed them, but I just wanted them to know I had their backs when need be.

We would play a game I called the "Hi/Lo game" at dinner on nights I wasn't teaching piano. We would go around the table and say our high for the day and our low. It was a great way to get them to talk about their day without being asked direct questions. When the kids were arguing with each other, I would sometimes have them come to the table, and I would have paper in front of them. They had to write down all the things they liked about their siblings on a separate page, then they had to do it for themselves as well. Each person would read what everyone said about them, and then they could leave the table. We didn't talk about what was written; it was just so they could see the good in each other instead of the bad. They always walked away happy.

They may not remember some of the things I did for and with them when they were younger, but I

Cut The Anchor

think that is the same for most families. We do so much for our kids, but some of it is just forgotten. I was also very overprotective, which may have upset them, but I just wanted to keep them safe. I had trust issues. I am still not sure where the trust issues came from, but I never let any of them be alone with males except for my dad. I still need to figure that one out!

Many trips were made to the hospital, including knee surgery, many concussions, ear problems, and more.

My kids were all quite easy to raise other than the constant fighting between my boys, but I realize kids fight and disagree. I remember many times the boys would be fighting downstairs. I would stand at the top of the stairs to try and figure out who was at fault. When I thought I had it figured out I would yell downstairs (yes, I was a yeller), and then the other one would come to the bottom of the stairs and say, "Don't yell at my brother." I would throw up my hands and roll my eyes, but it was quite comical. Being a single parent is hard for various reasons, but never having anyone to back you or take over when you need a break—even ten minutes— was one of the harder things for me.

Going It Alone

Then my boys entered grades eleven and twelve. That was the end of no wrinkles and grey hair for this mama. My one son started drinking at a young age, and I never saw it. I had been quite a naïve mom since I never got into trouble growing up. So, I didn't know what signs to look for. His brother drank, too, but not to the degree he did. He was always a very good person, loyal to a fault, and would give you the shirt off his back, but he got in with a bad crowd and ended up drinking, skipping school, and doing drugs. I am not sure what all he did for drugs, but I know he drank and got into fights. I felt he was hurting inside and that was why he was drinking and fighting, but I didn't know where the anger and hurt were stemming from. I got him into ADAC when he was in grade eleven, but you can't make someone get sober. They have to want it for themselves. I never had the support or backing from his dad as he kept saying he didn't believe that *he* was drinking or doing drugs. Even his brother told his dad about the drinking and drugs; however, he chose not to believe either of us. It was a very difficult time. I was worried constantly, never knowing if one of those fights would land him in the grave. But I was always there for him. I was just a phone call away. I did end up taking him to the hospital one time

Cut The Anchor

after a fight at a bar where he was protecting his brother. It really scared me, and I was at a loss as to how to help him. At age twenty-four he called me to tell me he had taken his last drink. I helped him through the withdrawal stage as he chose to do it on his own and not go to the hospital or a treatment center. There is much more on this topic, but I will save it for a book all on its own. What I will say is that I couldn't be prouder of him. He has been through hell and back and still has not taken a drink since that August 20th day in 2017. Over the last year, with everything he has endured, I believe it would have been very tough for most to not drink, but he has stayed sober. Have you gone through something hard like this with your kids? It is so hard to watch and not know what to do to help, other than be there for them when they need you.

It was tough when my kids moved out. My daughter moved out at twenty, and we had been so close that I cried every day for a year after she left. I didn't know what to do with myself; I was devastated—which seems ridiculous because isn't that what I raised my kids to do—be responsible enough to move out and be on their own? I was on holidays in Vernon when she texted and told me she had moved out. I had thought she had been asking me

Going It Alone

the previous three months, but I finally realized she had been giving me notice. Breaking me in slowly to the fact she would be moving in with her now husband. Five years later I went on holiday again (this seemed to be when my kids did big things), and when I came home one of my boys said, "Do you want to come and see my new house?"

"Your what?" I asked.

He had purchased his first home all on his own at age 21. I was extremely proud of him. My son who drank was the last to go, and I asked if he would consider staying. He did for a bit but then moved out—two hours away for work. I felt unneeded by my kids at this point, which is common for empty nesters—but I didn't have a spouse or partner to fill my time with, so I was very lonely.

Being a single mom was tough! I always wanted to be a mom. I know I made mistakes, and some very big ones, but I tried my absolute best to be the most loving, giving, caring parent I could be with the tools and resources that I had at the time. I felt very lost for many years, trying to find my place as a mom after my kids moved out. I still do not know my place with two of my adult children, and it has been very tough on me. But I love them all deeply, and my hope is one day to all be a happy family unit again.

There are resources out there for single parents, but you have to search for them. I found out from a friend that the county had a program for low-income families. I was able to get a subsidy for my kids to attend the recreation center where I lived. I could put them in any program offered and just had to pay 25% of the cost. They also had access to get into any recreation center in Sherwood Park, allowing them to skate or swim for free. Also, health care had a subsidy so my kids could go to the dentist and get prescriptions and glasses for free. I received subsidies to go to university plus other courses I had taken. Do your research to see what is out there to help with single-income homes. They are there. Sometimes you just have to search for them.

Once my kids were school-age, I made sure to take care of myself every day. I went to the gym from 9-11 a.m., and my kids knew only to call if they absolutely needed me. I also would go on a holiday each year without them. I got called selfish many times over the years by different people, but when you are a single parent with not much time

Going It Alone

for yourself and no help, it is vital to take that time to regenerate. If you don't you will burn out, and that's not good for you or your children. If you are a single parent and you feel like you are drowning—just keep putting one foot in front of the other, and be sure to celebrate the wins at the end of each day.

Try not to dwell on the things you feel you did "wrong," and instead focus on the things you did "right." Ask for help when you need to, and try not to let others' opinions of how you are doing bring you down. You know how much you are doing for your kiddos, that is all that matters. Nobody walks in your shoes, so they have no idea what you are going through. Being a parent is tough, and being a single parent is even tougher.

But what I have found is this: To be good for your kids, you must be good to yourself first. If you are running on fumes, you won't be any good to anyone, yourself included. Find even ten to twenty minutes to be completely alone—in the shower with music going so you can't hear anything else, reading, journalling, or having a bath with candles and music. Meditate, dance in your kitchen, or go for a walk. Just do something you enjoy kid-free each day. I guarantee you will feel more relaxed, happier, and lighter, and you will be able to handle everyday things much better. Try putting on makeup, nice clothes that make you feel great, or some lipstick or mascara. It helps you to feel human and not just an exhausted mama.

*She made broken look beautiful
and strong look invincible.
She walked with the universe on
her shoulders
and made it look like a pair of wings.*
Ariana Dancu

THRIVING, EMBRACING, EMPOWERING

Do you have or do you know anyone who has Tourette syndrome? Or have you ever seen or heard someone who makes funny noises for no apparent reason? Or twitches their eyes, nose, shoulders, or head? They very well could have Tourette's.

According to John Hopkins Medicine, Tourette disorder (TD) is a neurological disorder. It is also called Tourette syndrome (TS). The disorder causes repeated tics. Tics are sudden, uncontrolled vocal sounds or muscle jerks. Symptoms of TD often begin between ages five and ten. They usually start with mild, simple tics of the face, head, or arms. Over time, a child may have different kinds of tics that may happen more often. They may also involve more parts of the body, such as the trunk (torso) or legs. And they may be more disruptive to daily life. This I found to be true with my own TD.

The most common symptoms are uncontrolled muscle movements. They may occur in the face, neck, shoulders, torso, or hands. Examples include: head jerking, squinting, eye blinking, shrugging, nose-twitching, repeated foot tapping, leg jerking scratching, or other repetitive movements. Complex tics would include: pinching, sticking out the tongue or lip-smacking, touching things, or making rude gestures. TD also includes one or more vocal tics such as: grunting or moaning sounds, barking, tongue clicking, sniffing, hooting, saying rude things, throat clearing, snorting or coughing, squeaking noises, hissing, spitting, whistling, or echoing sounds or phrases repeatedly.

Tic behaviors change over time. They also vary in how often they occur.

Thriving, Embracing, Empowering

Not everyone with the gene will have symptoms of Tourette's disorder. If a parent passes the gene to a child, the child may not have any symptoms. If a daughter inherits the gene, there is a seven in ten chance that she will have at least one sign of TD. If a son inherits the gene, there is an almost sure chance (99%) that he will have at least one sign of TD.

From what I have learned over the last twenty-eight years of researching TD, I have found the following to be true with myself and my family members who have it. Many individuals with TS witness a decline in tics during adolescence and early adulthood, sometimes leading to their complete disappearance. However, there's also a portion of the population for whom tics persist into adulthood, and in some cases, even intensify over time. I've noticed that stress and fatigue tend to exacerbate my tics, a trend that resonates with others who share this condition. It's essential to recognize that the media's portrayal of TS, often depicting individuals involuntarily shouting offensive language (coprolalia), or repetitively echoing others' words (echolalia), represents only a fraction of cases. These symptoms are infrequent and not prerequisites for a TS diagnosis. Unfortunately, despite the condition's prevalence, TS remains relatively unknown to the general public. When I disclose my TS diagnosis, the most common question I encounter is whether I exhibit the swearing tic. This lack of awareness underscores the importance of educating the public about the diverse nature of TS, dispelling misconceptions, and further understanding the experiences of those affected by this neurological condition.

One of my first struggles was in elementary school when my Tourette syndrome first reared its ugly head. I wasn't officially diagnosed until I was twenty-seven, which made my early years tough because I didn't know what was wrong with me. I would twitch my nose and blink my eyes a lot. I was teased by kids in school, which was hard because I didn't know why I was twitching my face. I am grateful that I was popular in school; I hate to think how the teasing would have been had I not been. Tourette's is hereditary and 80% of the time the male gene gets it, but not in my family. I got it instead of my brother. My dad, both my sons, and one grandson have it. I don't have it to the highest degree; however, it is a constant daily struggle. I go to bed at night completely exhausted and sore from twitching all day. I have strained my wrist, my shoulder, my hip, my toes, my abdominals and more

Thriving, Embracing, Empowering

from twitching. I am in constant pain in my right shoulder, hip, and wrist. This brings on migraines, sore muscles, exhaustion, and frustration daily. I get deep tissue massages every three weeks, but even that isn't enough. My massage therapist goes as deep as she possibly can, but my muscles are so tight from twitching constantly, they never get a break, even when I am sleeping. A lot of people say to me, "I don't even notice you twitching." I don't know if they are just being nice or they seriously don't see it, but in all honesty, it NEVER stops. I am in pain all the time, it exhausts me, and it is hard to explain to someone why it is so painful. All I can say is flick your wrist, or shrug your shoulder, and then don't ever stop, as in EVER. Just keep doing that over and over. Then you may understand what a person with TS goes through daily.

The twitching can get into my trachea, which is scary because I literally can't take a breath until I calm the muscles in the trachea down. I do yoga breathing and talk myself into a calm state so I can breathe again. It twitches in the trachea and then the anxiety of it happening makes it hard to breathe. I almost didn't get a job one time because I was sniffing, which is one of the common tics and the lady interviewing me thought I would be sick all the time. In reality, I am very seldom sick. One time I was in a lounge, and right when I walked past a girl, I twitched my nose, so it looked like I sneered at her. The rest of the night she was on a war path determined to beat me up because of it. Many times, men have come over to talk to me because they thought I was winking at them. Nope, just Tourette's! I almost didn't get into teaching fitness because of my TS. I was insecure back then, and when my girlfriend suggested I become a fitness coach I said, "Hell no, I don't want anyone watching me twitch my face." I am grateful she kept pushing me to take the courses. I don't know where I would be without my fitness.

Fitness helps with stress, which helps the tics, and I am also able to talk about TS and inform people of the symptoms and what it is all about. I have had a few people in my classes come up and ask me what is wrong (meaning why am I twitching), and I appreciate it when they do. I recently had someone in my spin class ask if I was okay. It was because I twitched my face, and she thought perhaps I was having a stroke. I would prefer being asked directly instead of being talked about behind my back. When I was at the heart of my body-building days, I was told by my workout partner, who was a cop

Thriving, Embracing, Empowering

at the time, that all the other cops who worked out there thought I was a coke addict. I was mortified. He said it was because I sniff all the time.

I am hoping to shed more light on TS, as it still isn't talked about enough, and it really should be, as a lot more people have it than one would think. Do you know anyone who has TS? Or maybe it is you? Or maybe you haven't been properly diagnosed and you have questions about it.

When one has TS, they are much more likely to have ADHD, OCD, and anxiety disorder. Lucky for me, I have them all. Perhaps I should be buying lottery tickets with my luck being as it is. I just say I suffer from alphabet soup!

ADHD, which stands for attention deficit hyperactivity disorder, ranks among the most widespread neurodevelopmental disorders. According to research done by The Mayo Clinic, ADHD is typically identified in childhood, but this condition frequently continues into adulthood. Children struggling with ADHD often encounter challenges in sustaining attention and managing impulsive actions without any consideration of potential consequences. This disorder encompasses a persistent

Cut The Anchor

cluster of issues, including difficulties in maintaining focus, hyperactivity, and impulsive behavior. As ADHD progresses into adulthood, it can yield a range of repercussions. These may include unstable relationships, poor work or school performance, diminished self-esteem, and a host of other challenges. Recognizing and addressing the implications of adult ADHD is crucial in reducing its impact and making possible your improved well-being.

I wasn't diagnosed with ADHD until four months ago, but my life makes way more sense now that I know I have it. Growing up I always felt quite stupid. I couldn't read very well. I had to read the same sentence at least six times to retain what I read, and my environment had to be completely silent while I was reading, or I was hooped. I even took a speed-reading course just to get me through my grade twelve exams. But let's be honest, I still had to cheat to pass English and social because I just didn't understand what I was reading in the time frame given or what the question was even asking me. I had trouble sitting still in school, or anywhere really, and I still do. I go to a play, a movie, or a concert and I watch the people in front of me, and they never move. They look like statues. I am moving, fidgeting, tapping my hands and my

Thriving, Embracing, Empowering

feet the entire time, but at least now I know why. I interrupt people all the time, I find it hard to wait my turn, and I don't like being told what to do (but does anyone?). All of these things appear to others like I think I am more important than they are, and that is truly not the case.

I don't have a problem following a rule; however, it has to make sense to me. So, needless to say, I had a lot of problems in school and still do in other areas of my life because rules aren't explained in many situations. I don't like authority, and because of this, I became an entrepreneur at the age of twenty-seven, which has been a blessing. A lot of adults with ADHD end up being their own boss because it is hard for them to be confined, told what to do, or sit still, along with many other reasons associated with ADHD. In school, I had a hard time focusing on things, and again I felt stupid because of it. I still have a hard time focusing on things that don't interest me, like making phone calls, reading and filling out forms, and doing paperwork for my business. It all gets done, but it sits there for a while in my to-do pile until I have to get it done. And even then, I feel defeated because I have such a hard time understanding things sometimes. Recently I was at a self-development course, and I had to fill

Cut The Anchor

out a questionnaire. The sound guy put music on and then turned it up halfway through our allotted time. Instantly I could feel myself getting angry inside. Soon it turned into rage. This is because I couldn't read the form and understand what I was reading. I talked to him later and suggested that perhaps next time he could refrain from putting music on as I was sure I wasn't the only one who was feeling this way. I told him I had ADHD and it was hard to focus with the music. He simply said, "I have ADHD and it doesn't bother me." I talked to another participant, and he too felt enraged. So, we all experience things a bit differently depending on where we are on the spectrum.

But give me something I AM interested in, and I can stay focused for hours. I even forget to eat when I am hyper-focused on things. These are all aspects of ADHD, which I have just learned about recently. Another really hard thing for me is regulating my emotions. I used to get really angry and fly off the handle at something, and then I would have a hard time bringing myself back down from the anger. I didn't want to be angry; I just didn't know how to get myself out of those feelings. And looking at the issue after the fact, I never knew why I flew into the rage in the first place because it was never

Thriving, Embracing, Empowering

as big as it seemed at the time. I still have a really hard time regulating my emotions, but now that I am aware of it, I can work on it. Maybe that's why I got so upset about the carrot comment.

One part of ADHD that I had growing up, and still have, is impulsivity. I always thought that was the fun part of my personality, which I still do and wouldn't want to change that, but now I understand it better. Someone could call me on a Tuesday and say, "Hey, do you want to go to Mexico on Friday," and I would be packed and ready before the phone call was even finished. I like that part of me, but it does get me into trouble at times. But now that I know why I do it, I understand myself better.

I can listen to four different conversations all at the same time and know exactly what is being said in each one (if I am interested in what is being said, that is). My conversations are like following a ping-pong match—keep up or you will be lost. I also have a really hard time sleeping as I have thoughts firing at me at all times. I can be dead tired, and as soon as I lay my head down on the pillow, I am wide awake, thinking of at least ten things all at once. I keep a pad of paper and a pen beside my bed, but it is irritating when all I want to do is sleep. Lots

Cut The Anchor

of evenings I set an alarm to tell me it is time to go to bed because if I didn't, I would be up all night. I used to have a lot harder time relaxing than I do now, but that is because I have worked hard at finding things to relax myself. I go to yoga, read, play the piano, and meditate. These have all helped to relax my brain more.

My ADHD has caused relationship issues as well throughout my life. I appear to be inattentive (I'm really not; it just appears that way), and I am easily bored, so if the relationship isn't exciting, which I am in constant need of, I tend to leave because I don't want to be bored. I talk over people, which comes across as rude, but I can't help it. I try hard now that I know why I do it, but it is still a struggle. I believe it comes across to others that I think I am more important than they are, and that truly isn't the case. Hyperactivity, sleep problems, and constant effort to focus cause daily fatigue. Having just found out that I have ADHD has allowed me to be much more compassionate towards myself for all that I go through daily. I also have sensory issues. Loud music, lights too bright, different fabrics irritating my skin, wearing clothes too close to my skin, people breathing too loud, gum chewers, loud chewers, and loud talkers all cause me issues.

Thriving, Embracing, Empowering

On the positive side, though, I can see things others can't due to my spatial recognition being incredibly strong. For example, if you want to move a piece of furniture somewhere, I could tell you within a pinky width if it will fit or not. I have great intuition, and I am extremely empathetic and compassionate towards others because of all that I have gone through and continue to go through. I am great with numbers, and I can see things quicker than others. I make decisions very quickly because of the impulsivity part of my ADHD, I can get a lot more done because my brain goes a mile a minute, and I am creative because of my ADHD. These I feel are my superpowers stemming from ADHD. Again, I try to take good from a hard situation.

Do you have ADHD or know someone who does? How has it affected your life? ADHD has such a wide range of symptoms; I am intrigued by it all and am just diving into learning more about it now that I know I have it.

I used to think I had regular OCD, but I was recently diagnosed with a subtype called "Just Right OCD" or "Tourettic OCD" (TOCD). OCD, in general, is characterized by obsessions and compulsions. According to The Mayo Clinic, obsessions are intrusive thoughts or urges that trigger anxiety, while compulsions are repetitive actions to alleviate this anxiety. These behaviors often become rituals to manage the anxiety caused by the obsessions.

TOCD is a specific subtype that involves compulsive behaviors like counting, seeking symmetry, arranging things meticulously, repetitive touching or tapping, and similar actions. Unlike typical OCD, TOCD doesn't involve complex obsessive thoughts or specific fears. Instead, it's driven by an intense feeling of discomfort, like an itch that needs to be scratched.

This discomfort leads to behaviors like thorough cleaning and organizing. For example, I wash my floors daily to address this "itch." It's not about wanting things a certain way; it's a compulsive need to eliminate discomfort. If the behavior isn't carried out, the discomfort becomes overwhelming and persistent.

This sense of incompleteness continues until everything feels "just right." The compulsion, such as meticulous cleaning, becomes necessary to avoid the "fuzzy" feeling in my head, which can interfere with daily life. It's crucial to differentiate between a

Thriving, Embracing, Empowering

strong preference for cleanliness and this compulsive need for mental relief.

This need for perfection can be all-consuming and affect daily life and well-being. If you can relate to this, it's essential to seek help from a mental health professional for a proper evaluation and guidance on managing these feelings. When I am at someone else's home or on holidays I am relaxed, and I don't feel the need to have anything perfect. Maybe that's why I love going on holidays or having sleepovers at friends' or cousins' places. I don't have my TOCD symptoms when I am away from my house, which is common with OCD. Perhaps that is why I stay single—first, I don't want anyone messing up my place, but also who would want to live with someone with OCD unless they have it themselves? My boys both have it and have managed to cohabitate with their wives, but I know it hasn't been easy for them, especially at the beginning of their relationships. Perhaps that is just my excuse to stay single, which allows me not to be hurt again. I don't know. Can you relate? Do you go through the same things? How have you dealt with it?

The final neurodiversity I am blessed to have is anxiety disorder, which tends to go along with

Cut The Anchor

TS, TOCD, and ADHD. I started having panic attacks at the age of thirty. The first time I had one I was on a plane coming home from Vegas. I was by myself, sitting beside the window. The couple beside me put their trays down, and at that point, I started to get a funny feeling inside. I started to sweat, I didn't know what was happening, and then they put their laptops on the trays, and I went into a full-blown panic attack. At the time I didn't know what it was—apparently, I am claustrophobic and didn't know it. I need to know I can get out of a place easily, so having the trays down was bad, but once the laptops got put on top, my brain told me I was stuck where I was. That was the end of sitting by the window on planes. Shortly after I had the worst one of my life. It lasted two hours. I was ready to go to the hospital. I had an out-of-body experience, and I remember my dad telling me about one he had on the streets of downtown Calgary. So, I knew I wasn't going crazy, and I just had to wait it out. I was freezing, and my daughter, ten at the time, just had to keep putting blankets on me and sit beside me on the couch. I am sure it scared her looking back at it now. I had them a lot in my thirties. I had them at dance recitals, on the way to appointments, subbing fitness classes, teaching fitness classes after being off for the summer, or any extended period.

Thriving, Embracing, Empowering

Pretty much anywhere, any time. They stopped for a while, and then during perimenopause, they started up again, mostly when I was hiking, even hikes I had done many times previously. I use coping strategies now, which include yoga breathing (deep inhales and exhales), box breathing (into the count of four, hold for four, then out to the count of four), meditating, and journalling. It has gotten so much better over the years.

But having them isn't fun, and I am grateful they don't happen often anymore. Do you suffer from anxiety? Do you get panic attacks? What do you do to help calm you down?

Tourette syndrome is the umbrella, and underneath are ADHD, OCD/TOCD, and anxiety. Just because a person has TS doesn't mean they will automatically have the others, but there is a much higher chance of having one or more if you have TS.

None of these neurodiversities are fun to have. However, I am the woman I am today because of them. I know what it is like to be different, to learn differently, to understand differently, and to be looked at and perhaps judged for things I do or say. But I am also grateful for having these

Cut The Anchor

because I am compassionate, empathetic, and understanding to those who have differences. We all go through things in life, whether they are physical or mental or perhaps both. It is how we choose to have them affect us that counts. I refuse to let my neurodiversities define me. I am strong, caring, and kind, and I will continue to forge through this life with my head held high, learning everything I can about these neurodiversities. If you are interested in learning more, please reach out to me.

Everybody is a genius,
but if you judge a fish by its ability to climb a tree,
it will live its whole life believing that it is stupid.

Author unknown

INSECURITIES, FREEDOMS, HEADACHES

Have you always known you would work for a company? Or have you been like me where you knew at a young age you would work for yourself? I am not sure why, but I have always felt I was going to be an entrepreneur.

I embarked on my journey of independence early on, starting at ten when I began delivering newspapers weekly. Those were the days when customer

Cut The Anchor

collections were part of the process. My dad stood by, offering his support from the sidewalk, allowing me to handle the task solo while he remained a reassuring presence in case I needed help.

Simultaneously, my entrepreneurial spirit led me into the realm of babysitting. By the age of fourteen, I had established a regular clientele for my babysitting services, providing me with consistent work each week. My dad, ever the advocate of financial wisdom, initiated my exposure to responsible money management by having me open a bank account at age ten. The practice of setting aside 10% of my earnings into a savings account became a valuable lesson in financial stability. Although I approached the teller myself, my dad remained in the background again, a safety net in case his guidance was required.

When I was married the first time, my determination to have my own money led me to teach piano lessons and engage in Tupperware sales. Hosting in-home Tupperware parties became my way of connecting with potential customers, a method necessitated by the absence of the online platforms we have today. My second marriage saw a continuation of my multifaceted endeavors. My role as a piano instructor persisted, and I expanded my horizons by nurturing

Insecurities, Freedoms, Headaches

a dried floral business. Crafting arrangements by drying flowers either sourced personally or acquired from distributors, I ventured into sales at craft fairs and stocked my creations in various small craft stores around Edmonton. The process involved not only creating the arrangements but also engaging in the proactive pursuit of commissions by approaching different stores. Through each phase of my journey, the invaluable lessons from my dad's guidance and my own tenacity sculpted my path toward financial freedom and personal growth.

After my second divorce, I found myself stepping into a new chapter by joining a frozen food business, as I mentioned before. Observing the owner's lack of dedication to the business, I felt a deep connection and understanding of the business that surpassed his own. After running it in his absence, I approached him with the idea of purchasing the business. His willingness to sell marked the beginning of an ambitious endeavor, though I was about to encounter unforeseen challenges. Securing a business loan proved to be a daunting task, especially for a single woman lacking prior business experience. In those times, the skepticism towards women in business was palpable. The financial institution's offer of a loan capped at 25 thousand was a fraction of what was needed, yet I pressed forward with determination. My initial steps into entrepreneurship were marked by trial and error; I made mistakes but also absorbed invaluable lessons. The business grew rapidly, expanding from eight agents to twenty-five across British Columbia and Alberta in the span of a year. Alongside this expansion, the business underwent a transformation, rebranded as "Kari's Finer Foods." Acquiring the business thrust me into unfamiliar territory. Tasks like managing computers, ordering supplies, accounting, and working with others were uncharted waters. Behind-the-scenes roles had been my comfort zone until then, but necessity forced me to adapt swiftly. Establishing credibility was an uphill battle, as I encountered skepticism from suppliers, mostly male, who questioned a woman's place in the industry. Over time, my competence and dedication broke down these barriers, earning their respect and cooperation. However, the challenges were far from over. A Saskatchewan-based company, Schwann's, entered Alberta during my third year, siphoning a significant portion of my clientele. The immediate availability Schwann's offered resonated with customers who couldn't wait the two days it took for me to fulfill orders via truck to remote towns.

Insecurities, Freedoms, Headaches

The business's trajectory was a rollercoaster. While the initial two years were marked by triumphs, the last year brought forth substantial difficulties. In the end, the hardest decision of all loomed before me—the closure of Kari's Finer Foods. The finality of this step was tinged with sadness, as the business was a show of my hard work and a treasury of lessons. The journey unfolded as my sons aged between four and seven, and my daughter, ten to twelve. The feat of managing it all as a single mother remains a mystery, but my devotion to providing for my children fueled my determination. Looking back, I am a blend of pride for what I achieved and a touch of sadness for its closure. This chapter of my life epitomizes a single mother's resilience, embodying the spirit of doing whatever it takes to ensure the well-being of her children.

Subsequently, I ventured into the field of residential cleaning, which became my focus for a span of approximately five years. Juggling the demands of this endeavor alongside my existing commitments was a testament to my unyielding determination. On any given day, I would diligently clean two, sometimes even three houses, maintaining this demanding schedule four days a week. At the same time, I juggled various other responsibilities:

Cut The Anchor

catering, teaching piano, and pursuing a certificate program in interior design at the university.

This period of my life was marked by remarkable feats of multitasking and perseverance. My dedication to each facet of my professional life was unwavering, and I reveled in the autonomy that the cleaning business offered. I could shape my work hours according to my schedule, ensuring that the income matched the value of my efforts. Importantly, the nature of the business allowed me to be present for my children in the evenings, a vital consideration as a devoted single mom. Yet, the physical strain of house cleaning started to take its toll, resulting in a series of injuries that left a mark on my well-being. My wrist, hip, back, and shoulder all succumbed. While the cleaning business presented an array of benefits, including flexible hours, financial stability, and personal satisfaction, the cost to my physical health became too steep to disregard. With a heavy heart, I acknowledged that it was time to pivot once again. This juncture in my journey stands as a testament to my willingness to adapt and make difficult choices when confronted with the realities of the path I've chosen.

Insecurities, Freedoms, Headaches

My journey as a piano instructor began at the age of seventeen when I welcomed my first piano student. Over the years, I continued to expand my student base, steadily incorporating more students into my teaching routine. Initially a supplementary occupation, teaching piano remained a secondary commitment until I reached the age of thirty-four. At that point, I made the pivotal decision to transition into full-time piano instruction. The summer of that transformative year saw me planting a sign on my lawn, a small action that yielded remarkable results. In a matter of mere weeks, twenty new students joined the twelve I already taught, a testament to the demand for my expertise. Around Sherwood Park, I became recognized as the "piano sign lady." This period also marked the birth of "Kari's Kreative Keys," a manifestation of my commitment to nurturing musical talents. My teaching reached its pinnacle during the years overshadowed by the COVID-19 pandemic, from 2020 to 2022. The student count surged to a taxing fifty-seven per week, a feat that came at a cost. The transition to predominantly online instruction during the pandemic's first year presented its own set of challenges. Attempting to teach a five-year-old the intricacies of piano over Zoom proved to be a daunting task, testing my adaptability and creativity.

Cut The Anchor

While teaching piano remained a passion, I couldn't overlook the change in the attitudes and behaviors of the children I taught over the span of thirty-nine years. A shift was noticeable—some students exhibited more defiance, even rudeness. Additionally, navigating interactions with parents became more complex. The joy that once filled my teaching experience dwindled in the face of these changes. Consequently, I opted to downsize my student base, a decision that saw my numbers drop from fifty-seven to thirty-five. This shift marked a significant departure from my lifelong norm: two nights off a week. Sundays will still be spent teaching, but I eagerly anticipate experiencing what others engage in on Tuesday and Thursday evenings. With careful consideration, I've retained the students who share my passion for learning, aligning with where I want to be at this point. In this chapter of my life, my commitment to fostering musical growth remains steady, now enriched by the wisdom of decades and the understanding that transformation is an inherent part of every journey.

Throughout the years, I've embarked on various business ventures, including Scentsy, Tupperware, and now Tranont. The mere mention of "multi-level marketing" often draws skepticism from others.

Insecurities, Freedoms, Headaches

Yet, each of these endeavors had a purpose in my life—ensuring the financial well-being of my children and myself. The stigma attached to such businesses puzzles me, especially when the reality is that they have allowed me to manage my financial responsibilities effectively.

I've never been one to remain idle, a trait likely amplified by my ADHD. The idea of having multiple streams of income resonated with me. Earning my own money has always been vital, and the concept of "can't" never found a place in my vocabulary. People often questioned my journey, asking how I navigated unfamiliar territories or if I feared the prospect of failure. To them, I've consistently replied that failure was never an option in my mind; I simply couldn't fathom the idea of not succeeding. The driving force behind my choices has been the responsibility of raising my children. This sense of purpose has propelled me to tackle whatever challenges came. The journey was a blend of necessity and determination. It was a matter of doing what was necessary to ensure a stable and fulfilling life for my family. While external perceptions may cast a shadow on certain business models, my focus has always been on the concrete needs of my loved ones. My story stands as a testament to the power of determination, resilience, and a mother's unyielding dedication to her children's well-being.

Shortly after I got out of my frozen food business and while I was cleaning houses, a friend talked to me about becoming a fitness instructor. She was going through to be an aquatics instructor and said I should teach land classes. She had to work hard to convince me to get certified. I was adamant that I was not going to teach fitness in front of others because of my Tourette syndrome. I was quite insecure about it at the time. I didn't want people to see me twitch while teaching. But she kept at me to take the courses until finally I gave in and said I would register. However, I said I was only doing it to learn more about fitness for my personal information. I had no intention of it becoming my passion. Once I was certified I started teaching for the county, but soon after I decided to start my own business, and Fit2Motivate was born. At first, I just wanted to work with small groups of women. I felt the need to help women, and fitness was the starting point. To me, being fit and healthy and feeling alive through fitness is extremely important to becoming strong and empowered. I had just gotten out of that two-year abusive relationship

Insecurities, Freedoms, Headaches

with the man who only allowed me to go to the gym and I wanted to help women and myself to feel strong physically and mentally. I wanted to help women never get into an abusive relationship like I had, or if they were in one, I wanted to give them the strength and courage to get out of it. I did this for some time and have coached over one hundred women in their fitness journeys. Soon after, I also started teaching boot camp classes to larger groups. At one point I had twenty-five clients in my classes. I am grateful I am still in business and have weathered the storms that have come and gone over the years in the fitness industry. I am very grateful this friend kindly pushed me into taking the courses as I don't know where my life would be if I hadn't. I have met some incredible people through fitness that have inspired and taught me many things. Fitness has gotten me through some of my darkest days.

Recently in 2023, I decided to take Fit2Motivate a step further, and I now run goal workshops and fitness/wellness retreats, I teach many different fitness classes in person and online, along with accountability coaching. I even offer monthly memberships to pre-recorded fitness classes.

Cut The Anchor

So, if you don't have time to come to a class at a specific time, you can purchase a membership and access the classes at your convenience. I even recently created my app called Fit2Motivate. Check it out!

I am excited for this next step in my wellness journey. It excites me to inspire others to be the best version of themselves.

Success isn't only about what you do. It's about what you inspire in others.

Anonymous

Whenever you see a successful business, someone once made a courageous decision.

Peter Drucker

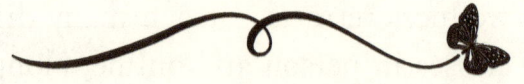

TRAGEDY, HEARTACHE, GROWTH

There are many definitions of loss, but for me, it is the absence of having someone here on earth and/or the absence of physically having someone in my life. Have you lost anyone you loved to death? Whether it was an accident, an illness, or suicide? I have many times.

Have you ever had a child decide to cut you out of their life? Twice? Sadly, I have.

Cut The Anchor

The first significant ordeal struck me with a force I could never have foreseen, a chill that lingers to this day. It was the frigid night of November 7, 1993, when my world teetered on the cliff of heartbreak. My seven-month-old son, seemingly battling more than a severe cold, faced a dangerous fate. My then-husband had accompanied him on that highway drive to the hospital. Due to the snowy weather, I made the choice to stay home with my other children while he drove our sick baby to the hospital. The diagnosis that it was a mere cold was out of alignment with my maternal instinct, an intuition that defies rationality. Once he arrived home from the Fort Saskatchewan hospital, I remained on high alert. I knew it was more than a bad cold. As the hours ticked away, my hand found solace resting between the crib's spindles, pressed gently against his chest, an anchor of warmth and reassurance in the midst of uncertainty. This night stands as a stark thread in my life, a reminder of how abruptly existence can pivot from ordinary to extraordinary, from routine to the surreal. And as the years flow by, that snowy November night remains etched in memory, a testament to a mother's bond, a son's resilience, and the fragility that underscores every heartbeat.

Tragedy, Heartache, Growth

Every breath drawn by his fragile twelve-pound frame was a struggle, a symphony of labored gasps that echoed through my heart. As the next morning arrived, my husband had already set out for work, leaving me alone to face the unfolding crisis. My son's awakening was an indication of terror—as I was changing his diaper, his eyes rolled back, and his complexion turned a haunting shade of blue. Panic surged within me, an adrenaline-fueled mother's determination to fight against the impending darkness. Gathering every ounce of strength, I collected my kids, my six-year-old daughter helping me by dressing herself and one of the boys. Urgency was our silent companion as I contacted my husband, setting up a meeting place on the highway, where I could pass off the two other kids and I could continue to the hospital. My destination: a hospital in the city, far from the facility that had previously dismissed our concerns. My voice resonated with the pediatrician, who immediately instructed me to bring him to the Grey Nuns Hospital. In that whirlwind, the fifty-minute journey transformed into a harrowing twenty-eight minutes, each tick of the clock increasing my anxiety. Once we arrived at the hospital, the pediatrician swept my son away, engulfing him in a flurry of medical professionals. The cold embrace of uncertainty wrapped around

Cut The Anchor

me as I was ushered into a chapel, where a minister's presence was meant to provide comfort but instead ignited a rush of emotions. Once I was calm, he explained that he knew I had no one with me, and he wanted to offer support while I waited for news. The weight of the unknown pressed heavily as minutes stretched into eternity. Eventually, the pediatrician reappeared, and her words shattered the silence—we were being transferred by ambulance to the University Hospital, which specializes in pediatric care. Unbeknownst to me at the time, his fragile life had slipped away, only to be brought back in the chaos of that emergency room's frantic efforts. The full extent of this traumatic encounter came to light as we were in the ambulance. The truth was unraveled in the information exchange between nurses during the NICU shift change. Apparently, an obstructed airway had cast a shadow over my son's fragile existence, a reality that required the insertion of a tube to restore breath. Once in the NICU, machines, tubes, and wires encompassed his tiny body.

During the clinical flurry, I called my parents, who set about on the three-hour journey while my husband's family never showed their faces at the hospital, other than his sisters for a mere thirty

Tragedy, Heartache, Growth

minutes. As days turned into nights, I never left my son's side. Fear mingled with fierce determination as I clung to him day and night, embracing him as if my touch alone could shield him from harm. My parents stayed with my other two on the farm. The aftermath revealed the fractures within our family. While my parents rallied, my husband's family's absence underscored the depth of their emotional disconnection. His return to work the day after the crisis, further strained our relationship, and the gap between our values widened as his priorities came into stark focus. It was at that moment I realized why my husband was unable to show his emotions: he was never taught as his family completely lacked them. I never truly forgave my husband for going back to work the day after, and I do believe it was the start of the end of our marriage. I had no respect for him, and I knew then that his family was not first, but little did I know that my daughter and I were fifth in line of importance. That came out during our separation.

The diagnosis—croup and tracheitis, an improbable combination—provided clarity to the tumultuous events. Bacterial tracheitis (they emphasized its rarity) mirrored the symptoms of croup but carried a much graver threat. In those uncertain moments, I clung to

Cut The Anchor

the decision to trust my instincts, a choice that likely saved my son's life. In the face of adversity, my resolve became clear: to listen to the whispers of intuition and to fiercely advocate for my children's well-being. That fateful day solidified the notion that a mother's intuition is an unwavering compass in the maze of life's uncertainties. Have you almost lost a child to illness or accident? Perhaps you have lost a child and if you have, I am truly sorry for your loss. Having something happen to your child is unthinkable.

The ups and downs of relationships, something we all go through, really affected me. Among them, the way my connection with my daughter changed hit me hard. Right from the start, we had this strong bond that made us more like friends than parent and child. It was all genuine, but looking back, I see it had its complications. As she went through her teenage years and into adulthood, I still viewed her as a friend and confidante. I didn't realize the weight of the expectations I had put on her until much later. The cracks in our connection only became clear as she grew older. We didn't have the usual parent-teen drama; her teenage years were pretty smooth. She was an incredible young woman, acing her studies, being respectful, responsible, and popular among her friends. Our relationship seemed great, or at least that's what I thought. It was only much later that I understood the hidden burdens she carried.

Her silence during that initial period of estrangement unveiled the truth—she had felt an unspoken pressure to be the "perfect" daughter, to spare me any additional burden. It was a revelation that shattered my perception of our harmonious connection. The realization that my pursuit of perfection had inadvertently cast a suffocating shadow over her world was humbling and painful. I now understand that my aspiration to provide happiness for my children was sometimes veiled by unrealistic expectations. It was born of a time when I was young, navigating the intricate maze of single motherhood, and struggling with the weight of providing for their essential needs. Yet, in seeking perfection, I inadvertently sowed seeds of strain and tension. An internal river flowed against the current of ease, as I battled against challenges with unwavering determination. In hindsight, the key lay in realizing that navigating life's currents could also involve surrendering and allowing the flow to guide me. I see I was in a constant state of survival mode. If the river was flowing down, I was walking right through the middle of it, going the wrong way. All I needed to do was stop, breathe, turn around, and go with the flow instead of always going against it.

The memory of that Mother's Day in 2019 still lingers. It had been merely seven months since my sister's passing, a time when grief held me captive. And yet, it was on that day that my daughter made the painful choice to distance herself from me. The wounds of that event remained etched into my soul, tainting even the celebration of Mother's Day itself. For seven and a half long months, I was separated from my daughter, her husband, and the joy of my grandkids' presence. The fracture ran deep, shattering my sense of wholeness in a way that only those who've walked similar paths can truly comprehend. Then, in an unexpected turn, October brought a glimmer of hope. She proposed the idea of us going to therapy, a lifeline I grasped with both hands, eager to rebuild the bridges that had been scorched. Week after week, we delved into the complexities of our relationship, seeking a path to healing. That Christmas, the joy of being reunited with my grandkids was a precious gift, a beacon of brighter days ahead. During those therapy sessions, a question loomed, though: "If we encounter challenges again, will we find ourselves here once more?" Reassured by the answer that therapy would be our refuge, I braved the uncertainty with newfound resolve. But life's script often deviates from our expectations, and in September 2022, the bonds of our connection unraveled once again. A secret, once concealed, cast shadows that drove us apart. Social media became a barrier, and my access to my grandkids was blocked. The pain of estrangement returned, a somber note that played on my heartstrings.

As it stands, the ache of separation persists. My daughter, her husband, and my grandkids remain a distant presence, the wounds of distance and estrangement carving spaces that long for healing. After six months, I was faced with the heart-wrenching task of dismantling the toy room that had once been a symbol of joy and laughter. Now an office, it has become a sanctuary where I pour my emotions into the pages of this book, a journey of resilience and reflection. Has a child of yours cut you from their life? Have you lost grandkids over a dispute or issue? How have you coped with it?

The intricate dance of family relationships has never been a straight path for me. My rocky bond with my sister mirrored the complexities I experienced

Cut The Anchor

elsewhere. Despite the strain between us, fate intervened one Sunday in May. Sadly, my sister and I hadn't spoken in over a year. Then I received a sobering phone call. I had just parked my car and was getting out to teach a boot camp class when my cell rang. It was my dad informing me my sister had stage four lung cancer and had been given eight to ten months to live. I was in complete and utter shock. I didn't hear anything he said after I heard the words "stage four cancer." I had to call my parents back after my class to see if I had heard him correctly. I was devastated. I called my sister right away and left a message. She called me back the next day and we talked for the first time in over a year.

I made the decision right away to go live in Vancouver during that summer so I could spend as much quality time with her as possible. My kids were amazing and helped me out with money so I was able to go and still pay bills while I was gone. They shared taking care of my dog Ruxton and looked in on my home. Also, a friend's sister who lived in Vancouver let me live in her basement for the summer rent-free, and it ended up she lived only a ten-minute drive from my sister. My sister and I were able to cross a lot of bucket list items off that summer: zip lining, a helicopter

Tragedy, Heartache, Growth

ride to a beautiful winery in Vernon, wake surfing, and much more.

We became very close, and I value every second I got to spend with her. We would meet with my brother at coffee shops, movies, and dinners where the three of us would laugh for hours until our cheeks hurt. I miss those days so much. I remember sitting at a coffee shop near my brother's work for four hours. We never stopped talking and most of it included nonstop laughing. I know people were thinking, "I want to be at their table."

In the wake of my sister's cancer diagnosis, the urgency to be close to her drove me to make a life-altering decision. In January, I made the bold choice to sell my home, seeking the freedom of a mortgage-free life that would allow me to cross the miles between us and be by her side during the rest of her cancer journey. It was a decision filled with hope, an act of solidarity with my sister during a time of uncertainty. However, reality had other plans. While houses on my street had traditionally flown off the market, my own house defied the norm. Nestled

Cut The Anchor

beside the golf course in a sought-after location in Sherwood Park, my home should have attracted eager buyers. In March, I set the wheels in motion, listing my house and quickly securing a new home for myself just weeks later. Yet, the journey of selling my former house was a marathon, not a sprint. November of that same year arrived, and still, my house remained unsold. I found myself straddling two homes, two mortgages, and the weight of financial responsibilities that strained my resources to the limit. With two homes to maintain, the financial burden began to mount. Juggling mortgages, house insurance, and utility bills for both properties, my situation became dire. The strain on my resources left me in a state of financial distress, scraping by on credit cards and confronting the looming spectre of debt. The weight of uncertainty bore down on me, and I struggled with the daunting reality of maintaining two households without the financial means to do so. In my pursuit of stability, I adopted a frugal lifestyle out of necessity. I sold possessions, returned bottles for cash, and sought out additional employment opportunities to make ends meet. Nights out became a luxury I could not afford. As I navigated the turbulent waters of grief over my sister's health, the strained relationship with my daughter, and the relentless financial pressure of two mortgages, I found myself plummeting to one

Tragedy, Heartache, Growth

of the lowest points in my life. The merging of these challenges tested the very core of my resilience. It was during this tumultuous period that I confronted the depths of my inner strength and determination, forging ahead despite the overwhelming odds stacked against me.

I grieved my sister every minute of every day, with each new progression of her cancer. When the chemo stopped working, when the cancer spread, when it went to her brain, and when she got the blood clot that ultimately ended her life. I cried every single day; I would cry from the minute I woke till my head hit the pillow at night. The only time I wasn't crying was when I taught a fitness class or piano. And even then, my eyes were moist pretty much all the time. I was so lonely during this time as I didn't feel I had anyone I could talk to. My mom and dad had each other, my brother had his wife, and I was all alone. A close girlfriend of mine moved in with her new boyfriend and pretty much cast me aside. Or that is what it felt like to me. I absolutely learned who my friends were during this time. I had another friend say to me a week after my sister passed, "You need to be happier." I was stunned at the insensitivity. It still makes me shake my head at how some people are so self-absorbed that they really can't see past themselves to what others may be going through.

My sister and I became best friends during her cancer journey. She became the sister I had always longed for, and I am forever grateful for that. We learned a lot about each other, we shared our feelings and our thoughts, we laughed, we told stories, we joked, but most importantly, we were together. She fought a courageous battle for two and a half years, and on October 17, 2018, she crossed over. I was so proud of her, and she became my hero. I know she is in a happy place and is no longer in pain. Like my tattoo says, "We only part to meet again."

The weight of grief is a complex and individual experience, one that cannot be measured or compared. I recall an encounter where someone attempted to gauge my pain against the unthinkable loss of a child, suggesting that my grief might be of a lesser magnitude. While it's true that losing a child is an unimaginable sorrow that no parent should bear, it's important to recognize that pain and loss come in many forms, each uniquely affecting the individual who carries that burden. Grief doesn't adhere to a hierarchy, a predefined order that dictates which losses should be felt more deeply than others. Such

Tragedy, Heartache, Growth

an approach diminishes the complexities of human emotions and the intricate web of relationships that shape our lives. It's true that the pain of losing a child is profound, but that doesn't invalidate the pain of losing a sibling, a parent, a friend, or even a beloved pet. Grief is a personal journey, and the depth of its impact varies from person to person. In times of loss, it's not about comparing grief but about understanding and compassion. We should refrain from quantifying the depth of someone's pain and instead offer our support and presence. Grief also doesn't follow a linear path; it's a turbulent and unpredictable sea of emotions that can be overwhelming. What matters most is showing up for those who are hurting and being a source of comfort without judgment or comparison.

When faced with the challenge of comforting someone who is grieving, the best approach is often to listen and be there without the pressure of having to say the "right" words. Sometimes, silence speaks volumes, and a reassuring presence can provide solace in ways words cannot. Grief is an ongoing journey, a dance between cherished memories and the reality of loss. Even as time passes, the ache remains, a reminder of the love and connection we hold for those who have passed on. In my own experience, I've

Cut The Anchor

found that my sister's memory lives on in countless small moments that mirror her mannerisms and spirit. These moments remind me that the essence of those we've lost continues to weave its way into our lives, shaping who we are and influencing how we move forward. Grief doesn't fade; it transforms, becoming a part of us, a testament to the profound impact of the relationships we've cherished. Have you lost someone you loved? How did you work through your grief?

Some may think losing a pet isn't as traumatic as losing a human; however, to some this can be a devastating loss. Their pet was their family in some cases. Ruxton was a Shih Tzu, Maltese, toy poodle cross. He was in our family for almost twenty years, and in August 2020 he decided his time here was over. I wasn't in town when he passed, and I was devastated when I got the call from my neighbor who was watching him while I was gone. I had just left the afternoon before. The next morning around 7 a.m. I got a call from her, and I couldn't understand what she was saying as she was crying so hard. All I could make out was the word "dead," but I didn't know who she meant. Once I realized it was Ruxton, I was just sick. The guilt of not being there encompassed me. I felt he died because he

Tragedy, Heartache, Growth

was mad that I was gone again. But my friends and daughter said he probably left when I wasn't there so that I wouldn't have to see him stiff and cold lying on the bed like he was when my friend found him. I miss him so much and probably always will. I still hear his little cry sometimes when I am in the shower. He used to cry because he couldn't see me behind the shower curtain. He had quite a big personality for such a little guy. If he didn't like me having company over, he would go to his food bowl and push all the food out with his nose and then proceed to move it all around the floor. This was his way of saying the company had overstayed its welcome and it was time for them to leave. In the end, he had doggie dementia. I felt bad for him when he was in the corner of the room crying because he thought it was the door and he couldn't get out. He was also deaf and going blind, but you would never know it. He would run around like a puppy sometimes, and then other times acted like he was 100 years old. I think about him all the time, and his picture is right on the kitchen counter so I can see him daily. Pets are wonderful and offer unconditional love. It is so very hard when we lose them. Ruxton had a very good life—but I was still unprepared and sad to see him leave. Have you lost a pet? Perhaps you have lost many?

Cut The Anchor

Over the last eight years, I have had many hardships, from the loss of my sister to friends to Ruxton and my daughter and her family. I have grown from these losses and am learning who my true friends are. I am also learning what I truly want in my life.

I have also learned about the part I played in past relationships. I have hurt others in deep ways, and I am learning to accept what I have done. We all cause hurt to others even if we don't know we have. Even if we don't intend to, even if we don't see it as hurt. But if it hurt them, we played a part in it, even if we don't want to admit it.

Have you looked at the hurt you have caused? Have you forgiven those who have hurt you? Or perhaps it is time to look at who you want in your life and who brings you love and joy. Maybe it is time to do some relationship cleaning!

Without loss we wouldn't know love, without hurt we wouldn't know joy, without complicated we wouldn't know ease, and without the dark, we wouldn't know light.

Tragedy, Heartache, Growth

*Cancer can change your body,
and it can surely take your body away,
but it can't have your spirit.*

Linda Wolters

*When you come out of the storm
you won't be the same person who
walked in.
That's what this storm is all about.*

Anonymous

RESILIENT, ENDURING, TRANSFORMATIVE

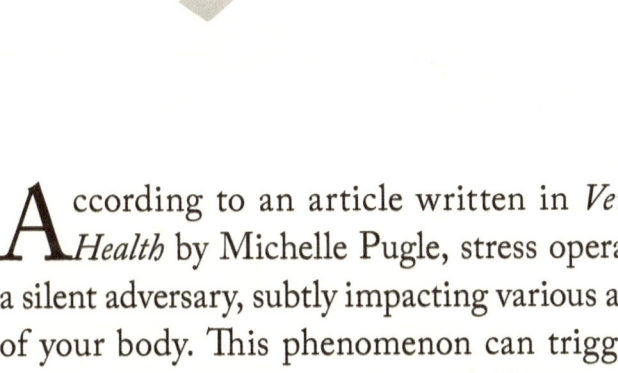

According to an article written in *Verywell Health* by Michelle Pugle, stress operates as a silent adversary, subtly impacting various aspects of your body. This phenomenon can trigger the body's fight-or-flight response, yielding a cascade of detrimental effects on your mood, immune system, digestion, and cardiovascular health. Neglected stress can act as a catalyst for numerous health issues, including high blood pressure, heart disease, obesity, and diabetes. While some individuals primarily experience psychological effects from stress, others encounter a range of physical symptoms, spanning from headaches to heartburn. This surge of hormones, rapid breathing, and escalated heart rate induced by stress can disrupt your digestive system. The heightened stomach acid production makes you more susceptible to heartburn or acid reflux. Furthermore, stress can disturb the regular movement of food through your digestive tract, potentially causing episodes of diarrhea or constipation. Nausea, vomiting, and stomach discomfort can also manifest as your body struggles with stress's impact.

If any of these symptoms ring true for you, it might be a valuable moment to embark on an exploration of your stress levels. Acknowledging and addressing stress can not only alleviate these physical and psychological burdens but also pave the way for a healthier and more balanced life.

The following is my story of the issues stress has caused for my health.

My upbringing was characterized by infrequent bouts of illness. Our home didn't seem to be a place

Resilient, Enduring, Transformative

where sickness was prevalent. However, a year after my daughter and I relocated to the farm where my second husband resided, I found myself falling quite ill. During this time, my health deteriorated to such an extent that I was confined to the couch, unable to perform even my usual activities, including work. This contrasted sharply with my typical disposition. The incapacitating condition persisted for approximately two weeks. When a similar episode recurred the subsequent spring, I recognized that it couldn't merely be attributed to a common spring cold. On this occasion, the sickness was more severe, prompting me to enlist my mom's help in caring for my daughter and me.

Consulting my doctor led to allergy testing, which unveiled my sensitivities to dust, mold found in soil, horses, cows, and cigarette smoke. Strikingly, these allergies manifested only after I moved to the farm. However, upon divorcing and relocating away from the farm, my sensitivities vanished, except for my continued reaction to cigarette smoke.

Based on my research and discussions with my doctor, it became evident that the stress stemming from my marriage and farm life contributed to my health struggles. After enduring two years of seasonal allergies that would invariably strike at the onset of spring, I eventually developed chronic fatigue syndrome. The realization of what I was facing hit me the year after enduring a particularly severe bout of allergies.

I was so extremely fatigued that I found myself needing to pull over on the side of the highway during my commute to work for a quick power nap of about twenty minutes every day. Even at my workplace, I was limited to light duties, as my hands lacked coordination, causing items to slip from my grasp unpredictably due to my extreme exhaustion. The drive back home was no different, requiring yet another roadside nap midway. My husband, upon collecting my daughter from daycare, would proceed to prepare dinner. I would rise in time to have a meal before sharing a cuddle with my daughter in bed, after which I would drift back into sleep for the night. This routine became an unvarying pattern.

I loathed my state of sickness, the relentless fatigue, the inability to engage in activities, the persistent ache in my muscles, and the sudden loss of control over my own body. On one occasion, while walking from the bathroom toward the living room where we were watching E.T., my legs abruptly gave out,

Resilient, Enduring, Transformative

causing me to collapse onto the floor and crawl the remainder of the way. My husband watched this unfold without offering assistance, convinced that I was feigning my condition.

I began to sign up for classes—be it fitness, dance, or a craft workshop—with the hope that committing to activities might motivate me to attend. Regrettably, last-minute cancellations became a norm, driven by my illness. My intention was to will myself into participating, but chronic illness doesn't bend to sheer willpower. What made matters worse was my husband's skepticism; he still didn't believe in the authenticity of my ailment. This lack of belief left me feeling profoundly isolated and unsupported, aligning with a recurring theme in my life.

I also suffered from migraines for twenty days each month. It was everything I could do just to stay sane. I am not sure if you have ever suffered from migraines, but it is horrible. I had them as a child, and then when I was eighteen, I was in a bad car accident and the migraines got worse. They lasted for nine years before I finally went to a chiropractor, and, eventually, he got them down to around three a month, which I could live with. I now have it down to maybe five a year, which I will take!

Cut The Anchor

Then in 2010, all my health problems started. I would be ready to go out somewhere and the pain in my stomach would bring me to my knees. I remember a few times my boys would come home to find me lying on the floor from the pain. It would come on so fast and last anywhere from an hour to all night and hurt to the point where I couldn't move. This lasted for a couple of years, and after many scopes, blood work, ultrasounds, and other tests with no results I decided to take myself off gluten. Within days the pain completely went away. At the time, I was very stressed from having twin boys in high school, and my son was drinking and skipping school. I do believe the stress of this brought on my stomach problems and the gluten exasperated it.

I seemed to be ok for about five years, and then in 2016, everything went to shit. I was running a race in the mountains (Sinister 7), and I felt great all day. Five minutes before it was my turn to head out, I started feeling sick to my stomach, but I thought maybe it was just nerves. Twenty minutes into the race, I started feeling sicker, sweating, and shaking, and I couldn't keep anything down, even water. I was dizzy and felt awful. I started throwing up, and it looked like a horror movie where an alien

Resilient, Enduring, Transformative

comes out of the person's body. I was throwing up a thick black tar substance. All I cared about was making it to the next transition so the next teammate could head out. On the way home the next day, my teammates informed me they had looked up my symptoms and one said, "I don't mean to scare you, but I think you were throwing up dried blood." Once home I went to the doctor, and she scheduled a scope procedure. It ended up I had a tear in my esophagus.

I had had acid reflux for quite a few years at this point and was on medication for it. But it now got so bad the medication wasn't working anymore. The food would get stuck on the way down, and the only way to get the pain to stop would be to regurgitate. Before this, I was sometimes able to get it to move down into my stomach, but now that was no longer an option. The only way was for it to come up, not down. Sometimes the food would be stuck for up to three hours, and it was extremely painful. I would just keep going back to the bathroom and try to throw it up. This ruined many family dinners and date nights. The food would come, and two to six bites in I would end up in the bathroom for what seemed like hours.

Cut The Anchor

According to research done by the Mayo Clinic, gastroesophageal reflux disease (GERD) arises when stomach acid repeatedly regurgitates into the tube that links the mouth and stomach, known as the esophagus. This phenomenon, referred to as acid reflux, can lead to irritation of the esophageal lining. While occasional instances of acid reflux are commonplace, chronic and repetitive occurrences can give rise to GERD. Fortunately, a majority of individuals can effectively address the discomfort of GERD through modifications in lifestyle and the use of medications. In rarer cases, surgical intervention might be necessary to alleviate persistent symptoms.

Because my medication was no longer working for me, it was time to figure out an alternative form of reprieve. I followed some great tips from a friend who had it: raise your mattress at the head of the bed, sleep more upright instead of flat, don't eat close to bedtime, limit or eliminate alcohol, don't drink pop, and eliminate acidic food. All of these things helped tremendously; however, it was still happening more than I wanted it to.

One time when I went for dinner with a friend of mine, I ordered a wok bowl, and he ordered a pizza.

Resilient, Enduring, Transformative

I took four bites and that was it for me. He sat and ate his pizza alone, and I kept going back and forth to the bathroom to get out my four bites, which you would think would take a couple of minutes, but that isn't how it works. So, finally, I said, "Let's just go. I will hopefully make it to your place." Nope, I made it to the truck and started getting sick beside it while people walked by. Okay, now I had to be done for sure! NOPE, our next stop was the liquor store—he liked to drink. So, he went in, and I stayed in the truck—oh shit, here it comes again. I ran behind the building and expelled the contents of my stomach. I laughed so hard after because the situation was hilarious. There were apartments right behind the liquor store, so if someone were to look out, they would see this woman throwing up right outside the liquor store. Is she making room for more alcohol? Or is she drinking it so quickly in the truck she needed to unload it? It made me laugh for days.

The worst time, though, was the year following my sister's diagnosis.

A friend and I went camping in Nordegg for a night, and steak, potatoes, corn on the cob, and salad were on the menu. I got down six bites this time, and it took four hours for all the food to get unstuck and exit my body the same way it went in. I was in excruciating pain and so uncomfortable. Plus, I was starving. But you can't put more food down when your current food is stuck. I can't even drink water at that point. Finally, it all came out!

That was it for me. I couldn't live like this anymore. I decided to do a reset with Whole30, where all I could eat was meat, eggs, nuts, seeds, and vegetables. I followed it for thirty days straight with no cheating, and what I figured out was meat is a no-go for me. It would get stuck every time, along with certain veggies: Brussels sprouts (but who likes those anyways?), green peppers (other colors are totally fine), broccoli, cabbage, and tomatoes, just to name a few. So, I decided to control my GERD through what I ate and not with meds. My food now gets stuck maybe two times a year instead of every meal, every day.

During the period when I was struggling with severe eating issues, I also experienced intense gastrointestinal distress (I find it challenging to use the term "diarrhea"). This compounded my struggles as I was both vomiting and experiencing significant digestive problems, causing me to lose

Resilient, Enduring, Transformative

a substantial amount of weight. At that point, my weight had dropped to 102 pounds, resulting in comments that showcased the double standard of body shaming. While discussions often center around fat shaming, it's important to recognize that skinny shaming is equally hurtful. People seem to feel it's acceptable to make fun of someone who is very thin, yet similar comments about weight gain are deemed rude. For instance, if I were to comment on someone's weight gain, the response would likely be negative, but when comments like "You're so skinny, eat a sandwich!" are directed at me, they're often brushed off as jokes. People may even defend themselves by saying they wish to be that thin, but I find this disingenuous. If they experienced the health challenges I've faced over the last decade, their perspective might be different.

My unsolicited advice to others is this: If you're genuinely concerned about someone's weight changes, approach the situation with compassion. Ask if they're okay and express your concern for their well-being. Alternatively, if you're unsure how to address the topic sensitively, it's perfectly fine to say nothing at all. Remember, body shaming, regardless of the direction, is hurtful and can have lasting emotional effects.

Cut The Anchor

I have had scopes, ultrasounds, colonoscopies, numerous rounds of blood work, stool samples, bile consumption scans, SIBO test, and much more over the years. These are the things I have found out from the tests: the muscles near the top of my esophagus don't work. They are dead muscles based on how it was described to me. That is why when the food would get stuck, the muscles couldn't push the food down, and therefore I had to throw it up. My weight has fluctuated over the last six years depending on whether I am in a flare-up or not. I am unsure at this point what exactly brings on the flare-up, but I do know most dairy is a no-go. But even that is hard to figure out because some dairy I can eat and some I can't. Also, what is okay today might not be okay tomorrow. So, it is frustrating not knowing what the problem is. But when the digestive issues were at their worst, I decided to only eat when I knew I would be home for the rest of the night. Therefore, my first meal of the day would be 2 p.m. because then I would be home teaching piano the rest of the evening. I made this decision after many outings where I didn't make it to the bathroom in time. The stress of not knowing where the bathroom is when you have to go RFN is horrible. The first thing I look for in any situation is the bathroom, whether it is someone's house, a

Resilient, Enduring, Transformative

store, or a restaurant. I was running trails in the river valley and, yep, had to go in the bushes. I was day hiking Berg Lake only to realize I forgot toilet paper (a bunch of large leaves it is). On the way to a massage, I shit my pants in the car. When I got to the clinic I ran into the bathroom, washed my pants and panties, and then proceeded to try and "relax" for the next ninety minutes. Another time it happened on my treadmill at home. I got good at doing the duck walk from the car to my bathroom in the house many times. I learned to laugh about it because when it is that bad what else are you going to do?

I eventually managed to secure an appointment with an excellent gastroenterologist in Calgary, referred by my cousin. His thorough approach led to a series of tests, including the SIBO test, which finally provided some answers by confirming a positive result. This led to a two-week course of aggressive antibiotics. Despite the treatment, my frequent episodes of diarrhea persisted. I diligently documented my diet, observing that foods once considered safe now triggered diarrhea. This cycle was not only frustrating but also frightening, as I became fearful of eating. I found myself limited to a monotonous rotation of just four meals. This restrictive diet left me malnourished, and the toll on my body was evident—my skin took on a prematurely aged appearance, resembling the sagging texture associated with much older individuals.

The physical toll extended beyond appearance; my skin became excessively dry, leading to dry eye syndrome. The chronic state of discomfort left me perpetually fatigued and struggling with persistent brain fog. This mental haze made even basic tasks challenging, and my ability to sleep and concentrate suffered as well. Each day became an uphill battle, marked by exhaustion, nutritional deficiencies, and a sense of constant struggle.

During this period, I began taking medications to manage my conditions, including TOCD, Tourette's, and ADHD. The decision to start medication for Tourette's was prompted by escalating tics due to heightened stress, while medication for ADHD seemed promising in light of my recent diagnosis. The ADHD medication brought a welcome sense of calm, and notably, I found relief from the compulsive floor-washing behavior that had been consuming my time. However, things took a turn for the worse. I began vomiting bile during the night, my sleep dwindled to a mere four hours, and I encountered

Resilient, Enduring, Transformative

a range of distressing symptoms—tremors, chest pain, headaches, dizziness, limb numbness, constant nausea, loss of appetite, extreme fatigue, and sores on my body. These challenges were coupled with worsening diarrhea that confined me to my home, aside from the times I taught fitness classes, which had also become stressful.

Adding to the distress, my weight dropped back down to a hundred and two pounds, which compounded the physical toll. At a breaking point, after enduring two hours of vomiting and sharp chest pains, I researched the severe side effects of the medications I was taking and was alarmed to find that I experienced most, if not all, of these severe side effects. This realization left me questioning why I had been put on medications that seemed to replicate the torment I had been enduring for the past seven years. Fueled by frustration and disappointment, I promptly visited my doctor to discuss discontinuing all medication. It was clear to me that the side effects had created a new form of suffering, mirroring the struggles I had been hoping to alleviate.

That night I decided that my health was completely up to me. It took two months, but I eventually weaned off all meds and started manifesting my good health.

Cut The Anchor

Every night I would meditate and visualize myself being healed, which I continue to do today. Was my poor health due to the stress of the last seven years? The loss of my sister? The loss of my daughter and grandkids? Was it because I was anorexic for seventeen years? Or was it something out of my control? I believe it was/is stress-related.

At the time of writing this book, I no longer throw up my food—but that is because I have chosen to not eat the foods that get stuck. I no longer have digestion issues nearly as much as I did, but it still isn't 100% better; it comes and goes, and I usually can't figure out what causes the flare-ups. I am not on any medication; I am choosing to be happier and not let stress get to me like I have my whole life. I am not perfect at this but a work in progress!

Have you experienced any illnesses that you believe were caused by stress? If you've had an illness that you think might have been triggered by stress, what steps or techniques did you employ to cope with that stress and promote your overall well-being?

Resilient, Enduring, Transformative

*When your body is filled with
stress and anxiety,
it's trying to tell you that
you need to make some changes.*

Author unknown

*I will breathe. I will think of solutions. I will not let my worry control me. I will not let my stress level break me. I will
simply breathe. And it will be okay. Because I don't quit.*

Shayne McClendon

THE BIG SECRET

Have you ever kept a big secret from someone you love? Was it due to fear of what would happen? Fear you may lose that person? Or some other reason altogether?

Secrets can destroy or come damn close to destroying a person's life. I know because it almost ended mine. It creates havoc on one's health, mental, emotional, and physical, and it can have lasting effects. It was a heavy weight that I carried for thirty-five years. Some memories have surfaced but not all, which is frustrating when I so desperately want them to.

Cut The Anchor

What I do know is at the age of nineteen I chose to have an affair with my high school sweetheart. There are no excuses; however, it was after being cheated on over thirty-five times by my first husband before we were even married. That is not a great reason, but it happened, nonetheless. I was feeling so low, depressed, unloved, and useless, and I was being emotionally abused by my first husband. I pretty much hated myself, and I just wanted to matter to someone. And at the time I thought I mattered to HIM.

I wish I could remember how we ended up getting together in the first place, but I truly can't. I have stuffed most of it so far down that I honestly don't know if I will ever remember the sequence of events. But here is what I do know for sure. It was the Tuesday after the May long weekend in 1987. I was having a shower before work when suddenly I started throwing up. I felt sick but not flu-like. I thought to myself, "When was my last period?" I was on the pill and took it religiously, never missing a day, but little did I know at the time, you can get pregnant while on the pill if you are on antibiotics. Off to the doctors I went, and sure enough, I was pregnant. Right away I thought, "Oh shit, is it my current boyfriend (first husband), or is it from the

The Big Secret

affair I had?" I only slept with him once; it couldn't possibly be his. Could it?

Things from there get fuzzy as I have a great ability to stuff things down and put them in a box deep down inside me. I compartmentalize very well. I know it is because that is how I coped with issues in my life up until that point. I had my daughter in December of that year, and I believe it was within four to six months that I was down in Calgary, my hometown. I was out for a walk with my daughter when HE happened to drive by. He stopped his car to come and talk. He asked who the little girl was, and I said, "I believe she might be yours."

His reply stung. He said, "Are you just wanting money from me? Because I am in a really good relationship right now, and I don't want anything to ruin it."

I was devastated, hurt, and angry. I replied, "No, I don't want your money. I just thought you should know."

I then went and talked to two people who I felt could give me some advice, but the advice was "Don't open up a can of worms if you don't know for sure." So, I buried it like I did most things and carried on with life. I was young and didn't know what to do. So, in October of the following year, I married my first husband, and I lived my life as if he was my daughter's dad. He and I divorced soon after in February 1989, as mentioned before, due to his final affair resulting in pregnancy.

While I set about on the journey of writing this book, I found myself drawn to a collection of letters, hidden away for thirty-five years, each bearing traces of a connection that had once been rekindled. Four letters, to be exact—sent on December 5th and 9th, 1989, January 3rd, and April 6th, 1990—marking moments when HE and I shared fragments of our thoughts and feelings. It all began with a letter from me to HIM in November 1989, a catalyst that set forth our correspondence. In these letters, I brought to the surface the threads of our interaction. In his responses, I discovered a glimpse into his world, his thoughts, and his perception of our shared history. My first inquiry to him was whether he still had that girlfriend, a question he answered with a simple "no." The exchange of words continued, revealing that he had journeyed to the Shuswap for New Year's, where he expressed a wish that I had accompanied him. Yet, by April, a different

The Big Secret

sentiment emerged, one that carried a sense of finality.

In the midst of our exchange, he alluded to my daughter by name, acknowledging he couldn't help but notice her smile—a detail that, to me, held significance. I couldn't help but wonder if he, too, believed that she might be his. The paternity question lingered beneath the surface, a silent inquiry left unspoken between us. A question that, despite its unspoken nature, had far-reaching implications.

Life unfolded, and I embarked on a new chapter, marrying my second husband—the man with whom I would have my boys. Yet, the shadow of uncertainty persisted. The echoes of her features—those fuller lips reminiscent of HIM—played on my mind. And her eyes, a deep brown unlike my own and my first husband's stirred the question once more. Could it be that her eyes carried the secret of her lineage? When my daughter reached adolescence, a biology class would inevitably raise the question. It was the moment I had anticipated and the one I had dreaded. I turned to a doctor, asking if the improbable was possible—could two blue-eyed parents produce a child with dark brown eyes? The answer was an affirmation of the rare, yet plausible, nature of such an occurrence. With this reassurance, I leaned toward the notion that my first husband was her biological father. Yet, the uncertainty, like a persistent undercurrent, refused to be fully suppressed.

Years passed, and the persistent tugging of doubt remained. The thought of HIM as her biological father gnawed at me. And so, I began my mission to find him. Through school reunions and the digital corridors of social media platforms, I looked for any sign of his presence. I ached to bridge the gap, to resolve the question that had lingered for so long. Despite my efforts, my search failed me—no trace of HIM emerged. It struck me that, in his role as a part of my life, long before our romantic entanglement, HE knew where my parents lived. An address familiar to him through years of visits. Yet, as the years stretched on, he never pursued that connection, never reached out to confirm or deny what lay beneath the surface. As I reflect on those thirty-five years, I contemplate the choices we make and the roads we take. Perhaps there are answers to be found within the unspoken spaces of our lives, within the decisions made and those left untouched. With each passing year, I confronted the absence of resolution—a persistent presence reminding me of the daunting questions that remain.

The Big Secret

Six months before that fateful day, my daughter brought up her eye color genetics again and said, "Wouldn't that be interesting if he wasn't my *dad*?" There, that was my opportunity to tell her the truth, which was that I didn't know for sure, but there was a high probability that he wasn't. However, I was caught off guard when she brought it up while we were standing in her kitchen, and I didn't know how to say it. So, I didn't say anything. I was a coward. I always knew deep down she would find out at some point, but I honestly thought I would be in heaven when she did. Again, hiding the truth was a cowardly act which I admit wholeheartedly.

The man she believed to be her father proved to be an inadequate parent, harboring racist tendencies and displaying a lack of empathy and emotional depth. He consistently prioritized others over my daughter, leaving her neglected mentally and emotionally. It's evident that she endured the distress of fearing abandonment and yearning for affection from an older male figure. This longing stemmed from her dad's inability to provide it, and it resurfaced when my second husband chose to abandon her at the age of eight. I empathized with her situation as it mirrored the emotions I struggled with throughout my own life.

Cut The Anchor

I beat myself up continually over this because I knew I had made a really poor choice. This secret ate me up inside, it cost me relationships, happiness, and my health, but, most importantly, it eventually cost me my daughter and grandkids. It was like the lie went on for so long. How do you bring it up, how do you admit you're a cheater, a bad parent, a bad human? This is what I thought of myself for years! It was in my thoughts every single day, just sitting there in the back of my mind, and never really seemed to leave. I lived and breathed this secret for thirty-five years.

The lead-up to the almost fatal day, Friday, September 23rd, wasn't great. A guy I had been seeing decided to stop talking to me and wouldn't tell me why. He had done this in the past, but this time it hurt more than the other times for some reason. I think because he meant more to me this time around. I was left feeling frustrated and at a loss as to what I had done yet again.

At this point, I still struggled with my limiting self-beliefs. So of course, I thought it was me. I was tired of feeling like I was always the bad one, the wrong one, the one not worth fighting for.

Then Saturday, September 24th was even worse—my daughter was angry at me for quite a few things,

The Big Secret

and she made it known in the parking lot of a CrossFit gym. I felt very judged, and I had had enough of being told all the things I did wrong. I felt nothing I ever did was good enough. I went home and completely broke down; I was just done! Done with feeling like everyone's punching bag.

I called a long-time friend and asked him to come over because I knew I wasn't doing well mentally. I took a huge leap of faith to trust another person with my feelings, which I was NOT good at. I trusted this person because he had been suffering from depression for years and had been suicidal himself in the past. I thought he would be the right person to put my trust in, but sadly that wasn't the case. He came over, gave me a big hug, and proceeded to listen to me for close to two hours. I sobbed uncontrollably and told him everything that had been happening in my life over the last year. I told him at least ten times that I wanted to end my life that night. And when I was done, he screamed at me and said, "YOU ARE SO ANGRY."

I said, "I am not angry. I am sad and broken."

He then said, "I CAN'T DEAL WITH YOU LIKE THIS," and he walked out of my home. I was in complete and utter shock. It reiterated to me that I was not important to anyone; I was unlovable and unworthy of any kind of love or compassion.

I proceeded upstairs, locked my bedroom door, and put a bottle of pills in my hand. I cried and cried for what seemed like hours until I finally fell asleep. The bottle fell on the floor while I slept.

Then September 25th, 2022 happened. Because of the issue my daughter and I had the day before, I was already feeling extremely broken, feeling like I could never do anything right in her eyes, or in anyone's really. So, when she texted and said she wanted to talk, I didn't have anything left in me. I told her I would call her later after my meeting or later in the week, which was out of character for me. If any of my kids want to talk, I pretty much drop what I am doing to be there for them, especially when I can tell it is something important. But I just didn't have it in me this time. I was barely hanging on. When I got out of my meeting there was an urgent text saying, "CALL ME, we need to talk." I knew something was up but had no idea what she was upset about. I called, and she informed me she had done 23andMe (genealogy) and that she found a 26% match with a girl. Which means the match

The Big Secret

would be a sister. My stomach dropped, and life as I knew it was over.

She told me that she had contacted this girl, and through a couple of emails or calls (I don't know which) she confirmed that she indeed was her half-sister, and she also had a half-brother. From what I understand HE knew my daughter was his daughter, and he had told his wife and kids about her. I don't know this as a fact because my daughter and I are estranged over the truth I kept from her. But from my recollection of the conversation that night, that is what I was told.

She wanted to know everything, rightly so. I told her what I knew and left nothing out—at least what I could remember. I don't recall my thirty-minute drive home. I was crying so hard I don't know how I made it home alive. By the end of the call, I was sitting on the floor of my back entrance sobbing when she said she needed time to think, to which I replied, "Of course, I understand." I thought it would be a couple of days or a week perhaps and that we would be back to counseling. But sadly, I was wrong.

That was our last conversation to date. I was so utterly broken after the phone call and the fight we had the day before that again I locked all the deadbolts, went upstairs to my room, pushed the dresser in front of the door, and took that same bottle of pills out of my nightstand. I am not quite sure what my brain was thinking by doing all of this, but I think I didn't want anyone to find me before the pills worked and I was in heaven. This time I took the pills out of the container and had them in my hand. I just wanted the brokenness and feelings of utter despair to go away. I took a few pills and sobbed for what seemed like hours, and, by the grace of God, I fell asleep again without taking ALL the pills. I awoke to them all over the floor. I was completely broken. More so than I had ever been in my entire life. And I have had some pretty low days. Five days later I was in Calgary at the self-development course that truly saved my life.

What troubled me about my suicidal thoughts was that I had this belief that you had to be depressed to want to commit suicide. And because of my history with depression, I knew I wasn't depressed this time, I was broken, which to me was different, so it scared me. Why then did I want to commit suicide? I talked to my doctor, and she explained that many people have suicidal thoughts at some point in their lives even if they are not depressed.

The Big Secret

She said it's just most people who have these thoughts don't act on them.

I tried sending a letter and a text to my daughter at Christmas that year but was met with uninterest in reconnecting or having a relationship. And I had to accept that to move forward with my life.

What I do know is that I did a really bad thing for what I thought was a good reason, but that does *not* mean I am a bad person. I made a mistake as we ALL have in life, and I now completely own it. It is through mistakes that transformation can occur. I did things out of desperation, fear, not having anyone to ask for advice, brokenness, low self-worth, and simply hating myself. This is not meant to diminish what I withheld from my daughter; it is meant to explain how incredibly powerful our self-limiting beliefs are and how they can destroy us, break us, and damage us beyond what we can conceive. I don't know if my daughter will ever speak to me again. I hope one day she will.

Through my personal development courses, I have come to the realization she was doing what she thought was right in keeping her kids safe and away from me. And by her thinking, I am a liar, which in all rights I was. She doesn't want me to hurt her kids like I hurt her. I now understand that. It was my doing that caused this, even though I was young and was trying to do the correct thing. I believe in my heart she isn't angry at what I did; she is angry at me for keeping it from her for thirty-five years.

I could say I wish things were different, and part of that would be true; however, if I had ended up with her real dad, I wouldn't have my boys, and she wouldn't have her kids or her husband. I wouldn't have the friends I have, nor would she have the friends she has. Our life course would have been completely different. Easier perhaps, happier maybe, but the what-ifs aren't how I live my life. If we live in a what-if, could-have-been, should-have-been state of mind, then we are living in a victim mentality, and I refuse to live my life that way.

My desire for myself moving forward is to work with as many people as I can to help them cut away those self-limiting beliefs. And to help them build themselves back up to be the best version of them. And for me to be completely transparent and authentic with my feelings and thoughts with those in my life from now on. And my hope for my daughter is for her to find peace within herself,

The Big Secret

forgiveness for me, and to find the love she has been seeking from the man who is her real dad. From my understanding, she now has a relationship with him and his family. This makes me very happy, but if I am being completely honest, it also hurts my heart. I feel that I have been cast aside with no sign of compassion for what I also went through. Which was making an extremely hard decision at such a young age. This is where the hurt stems from. Where are the hurt or angry feelings towards him, since he played a part in this as well? I will work through these feelings of hurt, and I hope that in time it will all be in the past. And we can be a family again, in whatever form that may look like.

Lies and secrets hold us down like an anchor in the sea. They prevent us from living fully and soaring to our true authentic selves. Have you kept an all-consuming secret? Do you live with regrets? Or perhaps you are the one who has been incredibly hurt when someone hid something from you? I urge you to cut the anchor to those secrets you have buried inside you. Until those secrets are unleashed, it will affect your health, your relationships, and perhaps even worse.

Cut The Anchor

*You never know how
strong you are until
being strong is the only
choice you have.*

Bob Marley

*At any given moment
we have two options:
to step forward or
to step back into safety.*

Abraham Maslow

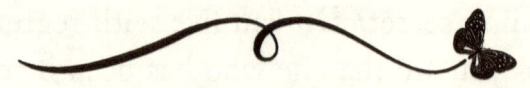

LIVING LIFE AUTHENTICALLY

Through this last year, I have been on a very spiritual journey of self-discovery. Five days after I wanted to end my life, I walked into the first class of my personal development course. It was the start of the new rest of my life. I attended several more personal development courses from September 2022 through September 2023. I have immersed myself in self-discovery and learning. It has been one of the hardest years of my life but, in some ways, one of the best. I have immersed myself in the work, attended in-person classes, and participated in over ten online courses, each lasting weeks. I have read the course books and completed the homework every week.

Things I have learned include realizing my parents have always loved me and wanted the best for me. They just showed and expressed their love for me in a way different from what I needed, but I do not fault them for this anymore, even though I did for most of my life. I have finally cut the anchors of resentment and anger and have replaced them with love, compassion, and the understanding that my parents did the best job they could with the tools they had. Just as I have done in raising my children. Lifting that weight off my shoulders has made me feel lighter, happier, freer and more alive, loved, cared about, empowered, and peaceful. Which is such an incredible gift I have given myself because I was living with so much anger. I am not sure if you have ever held anger or resentment towards someone, but it is exhausting and no way to live.

I have never done anything in my life out of spite or meanness; I have always done what I thought was the correct thing to do at the time. It didn't always appear that way to the outside world, but

Living Life Authentically

that is how I felt I lived my life. I truly never meant to hurt anyone with the choices I made. Life to me is about learning, growing, and being the best version of yourself with the tools you have at the time. Once you know better you can then do better, which has been my motto for most of my adult life. I always wanted to be loved and feel important, which I believe is how most, if not all, of us feel. Through this past year I have come to the true realization that until I completely loved myself and was important to myself, I could never receive that from someone else. Love must come from within. I have completely forgiven myself for a decision I made at a young age. I was young, scared, and broken, and I no longer beat myself up about this decision.

I made it out of love, not out of wanting to hurt anyone. Life is a journey, and it is what we make of that journey that counts. I believe we are given lessons in many different forms throughout our lives until we finally learn what we are supposed to. We all carry secrets, shame, embarrassment, or limiting beliefs about ourselves. I don't believe anyone is immune to these things. But it is how we choose to deal with them. Do we hide it away, stuff it down, or pretend it never happened? Or do we rise up and fix it, hit it head-on, and walk with our heads held high? I chose the first way for thirty-five years, and now moving forward I am going to choose the second way.

This is what I have learned about myself through this year of immense transformation.

I am compassionate and empathetic, and I want the best for those I care about. I am inclusive, a hard worker, and resilient. I am loving and now know how to show it and say it to those I love and care about. I know I deserve to be loved and cared about by friends, family, and someday a partner. What I am *not* is perfect, broken, unlovable, mean-spirited, hurtful, and alone.

Yes, a big part of my takeaway from my journey is that I am not alone, nor do I ever need to feel alone again. I have amazing people in my life. All I need to do is ask for help, and they will be there for me. This is something I never knew how to do in the past, and, as crazy as it sounds, a plywood wall is what taught me this. We all need people in

Living Life Authentically

our lives to pull us up when we are down, listen to us when we need to be heard, sit with us when we feel broken, and hug us when we need to feel loved or cared about. The right people will always be there for us when we are down.

We all make mistakes, but the important part is what we do with those mistakes. Do we blame others, retreat from others, or bury our heads in the sand? Do we turn to substance abuse, gambling, infidelities, or self-harm? Or put ourselves down with self-deprecating words? Or do we see the lessons we need to learn? Do we grow from our mistakes? Do we own them, seek the understanding to move past them, or, better yet, through them?

I have made many mistakes, some small and some undeniably huge, but I now own them, all of them, the small, the bad, and the truly ugly ones. And now I am living my life, putting the pieces of myself back together, finding my true place in this world, and surrounding myself with those who truly care about who the real Kari is, faults and all.

Do I have hatred or bitterness towards anyone from my past? A year ago, I would have said a big HELL YES, especially to the person I trusted with the

Cut The Anchor

fact I wanted to die who left me alone, but today I can truly say no. I own what I have done, and I own my self-limiting beliefs that I lived with my entire life until now. I know the part I played in the relationships with all the people in my life that I have felt hurt by. I also feel remorse for those that I have hurt in the past, whether the hurt was small or insurmountably huge. I know what I need to work on, and I continue to do so. I will continue to be a work in progress until my ashes are scattered on my favourite mountain and I am reunited with my sister and all the other angels that watch over me daily.

I have always had this nagging feeling that I was meant for more. I now know I was brought into this world to help others see their true potential, to stretch the boundaries of that so-called box they have placed themselves in from their self-limiting beliefs. To help others see that fear is what keeps a person in the safe box, the comfort zone, the predictable. But fear holds us back from living a truly authentic and amazing life. I hope that others will resonate with something I have gone through and will realize they are not alone and that your past does not define you. We are all human, and humans make mistakes. It is how we handle those mistakes that count. Do we hide from them, lie

Living Life Authentically

about them, or bury them, or do we own them and choose to make them right?

The loss of my daughter and my grandkids has been extremely hard, but I chose to take this time to work on myself and to become a better human. To see exactly what part I played in the loss that almost killed me on September 25th. I had to take a really hard look at myself and take full responsibility for the part I played in everything that has happened to me in my life. But I have done it and will continue to do it moving forward. All the mistakes I have made, the insecurities I had from childhood that followed me into adulthood, and parenting. The lies I told, the hurts I caused, the anger I cast on others, and the defensiveness that I had for most of my life. The chip I had on my shoulder for years, the silent treatment I gave to friends and family. I OWN THEM ALL. And I choose to be better now that I have the tools to do so.

Will I make mistakes? Absolutely. Will I have setbacks? You bet. But will I own them and work on them? Every step of the way!

Over time, I have realized that all the hardships, heartaches, neurodiversities, and mistakes I have made have shaped me into the strong, independent, compassionate, empathetic, caring, and resilient woman that I can confidently call myself today. What a journey this life has been and will continue to be!

*Every test in our life makes
us bitter or better.
Every problem comes to
break us or make us.
The choice is ours whether we become
VICTIM or VICTOR.*

Lorenzo Dozier

*Though no one can go back and make a
new start,
Anyone can start from now and make
a brand-new end!*

Carl Bard

And finally!

Your past does not define you!!

ABOUT THE AUTHOR

Kari Berridge is a single mother to three imperfectly perfect children and grandmother to four amazing grandkids. She grew up in Calgary, AB, Canada in a family of three siblings and two caring parents. She left Calgary at the age of eighteen and moved to Edmonton, AB. After moving around the area, she settled in Sherwood Park, AB where she still resides.

Kari has been on a journey of self-discovery since the age of thirty-four after getting away from an abusive relationship. Kari has many neurodiversities, including Tourette syndrome, ADHD, TOCD, and anxiety disorder. And because of this, she has extreme compassion and empathy towards others who face challenges in their lives.

Kari has several businesses including a fitness business and a goal-achieving workshop business. She also runs fitness retreats, is an accountability coach, and teaches piano.

Her passion is to help others, along with herself, to be the best version of themselves. She coaches from a place of empathy, compassion, and intuition. She has thirty-nine years of experience with teaching piano and nineteen years of coaching in the fitness industry. She has helped coach over one hundred women to become the best version of themselves. She strives to live by example, committing to constant growth in herself while helping others to see their true potential. Resilience is her middle name. She handles whatever comes at her with grace, strength, and humor. Her motto is "Be the best Kari you can."

Kari Berridge

Kari Berridge embodies resilience and inspires transformation. A dedicated mother, successful business owner, author, and accomplished fitness coach, Kari's life journey is a testament to overcoming life's challenges. She is a passionate advocate and educator dedicated to promoting neurodiversity, breaking stigmas, and fostering understanding. Kari's expertise encompasses ADHD, Tourette Syndrome, "Just right" OCD, and anxiety disorders, and she offers a fresh perspective on these often misunderstood conditions.

Kari's impactful presentations, each lasting from 30 minutes to 90 minutes, as well as half or full-day sessions, cover a range of crucial topics.

1. "Cut The Anchor: Breaking Free from Emotional Baggage"
   - Conquering guilt and living fearlessly
   - Overcoming self-limiting beliefs
   - A journey from anorexia, depression, and toxic relationships to triumph

2. "Living Well with Neurodiversity"
   - Dispelling misconceptions about ADHD, "Just right" OCD, Tourette's and anxiety
   - Harnessing strengths and talents that often accompany neurodiversity
   - Promoting inclusivity and understanding

3. "The Resilience Road Map: Transforming Trauma into Superpower"
   - Turning past trauma into a source of strength
   - Navigating life's challenges with grace and determination
   - Empowering individuals to rise above adversity

Kari's unique blend of personal experiences and practical strategies makes her presentations both engaging and transformative. Her message is a beacon of hope, showcasing the potential for individuals to triumph over adversity and thrive.

For pricing, and availability or to book Kari Berridge as your keynote speaker, contact her at kari@fit2motivate.net and embark on a journey toward a more inclusive, empathetic, and neurodiverse future.

ACKNOWLEDGMENTS

I have to start by thanking my parents Lynn and Shari Berridge. I was nervous for you to read the first chapter of my book. I decided to read the first chapter to you with trepidation and I was met with support and love. This helped me to continue. I love you both.

Next, I want to thank my son Cody and his wife Trystanne for helping me through some tough times this past year and supporting and encouraging me through my author journey. Your love and support mean the world to me.

Finally, I would like to thank Natasa and Stuart Denman; Natasa is an award-winning author, speaker, and creator of Ultimate 48 Hour Author. Thank you to Stuart, who encouraged me with the chapters that were gut-wrenching to write. Your continued words of encouragement kept me going knowing I was on the correct path. Thank you both for putting on a great Author Retreat and for helping me see my dream through.

Thank you.

3 OFFERS WITH CALL TO ACTION

Unlock Your Potential: Dive into the world of self-improvement today! Head over to Kari Berridge's inspiring website at https://fit2motivate.net under the "Contact Us" section send a message with the subject line "BONUS CONTENT." In return, receive a FREE personalized plan designed to boost your self-esteem by dismantling those self-limiting beliefs. Don't wait; your journey to self-confidence begins now!

Cut The Anchor

Elevate Your Fitness Game: Ready to transform your workouts? Explore Kari's website at https://fit2motivate.net and treat yourself to a set of 4 dynamic short workout videos titled "The Magic Bullet" with Kickin' It with Koach Kari. Each video targets different aspects of your fitness journey – from full-body **strength training** to **core improvement, guided meditation,** and **muscle rejuvenation.** Elevate your fitness routine and order these transformative videos today!

Personalized Accountability Coaching: Take charge of your well-being with a one-on-one accountability coaching session led by Kari herself. Visit Kari's website at https://fit2motivate.net and book your exclusive coaching session now. Elevate your life, achieve your goals, and discover your true potential with expert guidance tailored just for you. Your path to holistic well-being begins here!

I can be found at https://linktr.ee/fit2motivatekari

BOOK REVIEW

A journey of letting go, forgiveness, and ultimately transformation. *Cut the Anchor* takes us through a winding path of healing that ultimately uncovers a courageous and brave soul who went from surviving to thriving, even after a deluge of setbacks, betrayals, losses, and heartbreaks.

Kari's authentic, heartfelt, and powerful story is so touching. This book had me rooting for Kari the whole way through and ultimately cheering her on as she transforms into the beautiful, resilient, forgiving soul she is today. Go, Kari!!

By Janessa Gazmen, Author of *Little Yogis, Big Feelings*

NOTE FROM THE AUTHOR

This book is a work of creative nonfiction, meticulously composed from Kari's recollections. While rooted in actuality, the names of individuals have been deliberately omitted to safeguard their confidentiality. The contents of this book are Kari's interpretation of past events, inspired by her genuine recollection. They consist of Kari's personal viewpoints and reflections, and no harmful motives are present. She anticipates varied emotional responses to this book; it honors the perspectives of all.

CUT THE ANCHOR BOOK CLUB QUESTIONS

1. In Chapter One, the author reflects on her lifelong struggle with feelings of not being good enough and the impact of self-limiting beliefs. Have you ever experienced similar feelings of inadequacy or self-doubt in your own life? How have these feelings influenced your decisions and actions?

2. The author discusses the role of family dynamics, labels, and words in shaping her self-perception. Were there any moments or experiences in your own life where family dynamics or labels had a significant impact on your self-esteem and self-belief? How did you navigate or overcome these challenges?

3. The author describes her journey through an eating disorder, highlighting the gradual progression from a desire to lose a few pounds to a severe struggle with anorexia. Have you or someone you know ever faced a similar progression toward an eating disorder or an unhealthy obsession with body image or weight? How did it impact your life or theirs, and what steps were taken to address the situation?

4. In Chapter 3, the author shares her personal journey through postpartum depression and depression. How did her experiences and emotions resonate with you, or how did they challenge your preconceptions about mental health?
Were there any moments or feelings described that you found particularly relatable or eye-opening?

5. The author discusses the stigma associated with mental health issues and the reluctance many people feel about disclosing their struggles. How can we, as individuals and as a society, work to reduce this stigma and create a more supportive environment for those dealing with depression or postpartum depression? Share your thoughts on how open conversations about mental health can contribute to positive change.

Cut the Anchor Book Club Questions

6. The author candidly shares her experiences with infidelity, both as someone who has been cheated on and as someone who has engaged in infidelity herself. How do you think her experiences with infidelity have shaped her understanding of relationships and her own sense of self-worth? Can you relate to any of her feelings or experiences?

7. The author delves into her own insecurities, low self-esteem, and the choices she made during difficult times in her life. Have you ever experienced a period in your life where you made choices that went against your values or lowered your self-esteem? How did you eventually find the strength to heal and grow from those experiences? Share any personal insights or strategies you have used to overcome challenges and regrets.

8. Throughout the book, the author shares her journey through a series of challenging relationships with men. What insights did you gain from the author's experiences in terms of how our past relationships shape our choices of partners? How do you think these experiences impacted the author's understating of love and self-worth?

9. The author opens up about the difficulties she faced in friendships, including instances of feeling left out and even betrayed by those she considered friends. How do these experiences resonate with your own encounters in friendship? Can you share any personal stories where you've had to navigate similar challenges? What strategies and lessons from the author's journey can be applied to foster more inclusive and supportive relationships in your own life?

10. Many single parents face numerous challenges, as described by the author. If you are a single parent, have you experienced similar challenges, and how did you cope with them? If you haven't been a single parent, do you know someone who has, and how have you seen them navigate these difficulties?

11. The author emphasizes the importance of self-care for single parents to avoid burnout.
How do you personally practice self-care, whether you're a parent or not? What are some effective ways for single parents to find moments of self-care amidst their busy lives? Have you ever faced a situation where you had to balance self-care with your responsibilities, and how did you manage it?

Cut the Anchor Book Club Questions

12. The author discusses the positive aspects of neurodiversity, such as spatial recognition, intuition, creativity, and empathy. Can you think of examples from your own life or experiences where neurodiversity has brought unique strengths or perspectives to a situation? How can we better recognize and leverage these strengths in ourselves and others?

13. The author emphasizes the importance of creating a more inclusive and accepting society for neurodiversity. What specific actions or changes can communities, workplaces, or schools implement to foster a more inclusive environment for people with diverse neurological conditions?

www.ingramcontent.com/pod-product-compliance
Lightning Source LLC
Chambersburg PA
CBHW030108100526
44591CB00009B/329